D1170312

JUEGO DE NIÑOS

Víctor Ruiz Iriarte

JUEGO DE NIÑOS

comedia en tres actos

Víctor Ruiz Iriarte

Edited
with Introduction, Notes, Pattern Drills, Exercises, and Vocabulary
by

Isabel Magaña Schevill
Stanford University

PRENTICE-HALL, INC.
Englewood Cliffs, New Jersey

PRENTICE-HALL INTERNATIONAL, INC., *London*
PRENTICE-HALL OF AUSTRALIA, PTY., LTD., *Sydney*
PRENTICE-HALL OF CANADA, LTD., *Toronto*
PRENTICE-HALL OF INDIA (PRIVATE) LTD., *New Delhi*
PRENTICE-HALL OF JAPAN, INC., *Tokyo*

Dedico esta edición a mi madre

I.M.S.

© 1965 by Prentice-Hall, Inc., Englewood Cliffs, N.J.

All rights reserved. No part of this book may be reproduced in any form, by mimeograph or any other means, without permission in writing from the publishers.

Library of Congress Catalog Card Number: 65-10071

Printed in the United States of America
[P-51217]

Preface

Juego de niños by the contemporary Spanish dramatist Víctor Ruiz Iriarte is a delightfully amusing, yet appealingly sensitive comedy which won the coveted "Premio Nacional de Teatro" in 1952. In addition to its recognized literary merit, this play is also an ideal source for intensive and extensive language study—from "pattern drills" to a full-scale stage production—because of its wealth of basic, high frequency constructions, its natural, witty, easy-flowing dialogue which is neither formally literary nor regionally colloquial, and its lively dramatic situations.

The author of this edition has for many years made use of this dual potential in teaching contemporary Spanish plays of this type, including *Juego de niños*, which was produced in Spanish at Stanford University. With this in mind, the present edition has been devised both as a reader and as an intensive language text for intermediate college Spanish and intermediate or advanced high school Spanish.

The purpose of the Oral Pattern Drills and Exercises is to provide the maximum opportunity for supervised and controlled class drills with the basic, high frequency constructions from the play. The Pattern Drills, used with the Verb Index Table, are primarily teacher-student class drills and do not depend on mechanical devices or the use of a language laboratory for their effectiveness—which of course does not preclude the invaluable utilization of tape recorders for adaptable procedures. It is hoped that the extensive, flexible drills and additional techniques given here may help to stimulate the almost exclusive use of the "foreign language" with the play, thus rendering unnecessary the procedure of translating from Spanish into English.

The Introduction includes an analysis of the basic themes and dramatic techniques in the plays of this distinguished representative of the Contemporary Spanish Theater. The literary analysis, together with the Supplementary Techniques and Activities in the Appendix, furnishes additional material for a more inclusive and flexible linguistic-cultural-literary aim.

Footnotes are given a free, contextual translation in keeping with the spirit of the play. Accentuation has been made to conform with the latest ruling in 1952 of the Spanish Academy.

I wish to express my deep gratitude to the author, Víctor Ruiz Iriarte, for his gracious permission to edit *Juego de niños*, and especially to Professor John V. Falconieri and to Dr. Edmundo García-Girón, Director of the Prentice-Hall, Inc. Modern Language Department, for their help in preparing this text. My sincere thanks also to Mrs. Elsa M. Staley and Mr. Leonard E. McCord for their professional opinion on the effectiveness of the Oral Pattern Drills and Exercises for both high school and college Spanish classes.

I.M.S.

Table of Contents

Introduction

Ruiz Iriarte and the Spanish Contemporary Theater

It is typical of the Spanish playwright Víctor Ruiz Iriarte that when asked for autobiographical data he should state quite simply: "Nací en Madrid, el día 24 de abril de 1912, y estudié en el Colegio de los Hermanos Maristas." But to this modest statement one must add a life of devotion to his dramatic art which begins in 1943 with the stage production of *Un día en la gloria* and encompasses, to date, over two dozen original and highly successful plays, some of which have been translated into Dutch, English, German, Italian, and Portuguese. In addition, he has translated and freely adapted dramatic works from Shakespeare, Terence Rattigan, André Roussin, Lajos Zilahy and others, contributed to major literary journals in Spain, and collaborated in the preparation of a number of movie scripts.

Ruiz Iriarte has won two major prizes coveted by all Spanish dramatists: the "Premio Piquer" of the Spanish Royal Academy for his comedy *Academia de amor* in 1946, and the "Premio Nacional de Teatro" in 1952, awarded to the outstanding play of the year, for his delightful comedy *Juego de niños*. *Socio de honor* of the *Círculo de Bellas Artes* of Madrid, *Socio de mérito* of the famous *Ateneo*, and member of the *Instituto Internacional de Teatro*, Ruiz Iriarte has also served as President of the *Sociedad de Autores de España*—ample proof of the respect and high esteem in which he is held by his literary colleagues.

Although his comedies and farces are original, one may find in them traces that betray influences of such playwrights as Alejandro

Casona,[1] Carlos Arniches, Jardiel Poncela, Jacinto Benavente, George Bernard Shaw, and André Roussin. In the *autocrítica* of some of his comedies and farces, the author frequently expresses his own views on the theater as a medium of joy and playfulness mixed with poetry, tenderness, and understanding. Most critics classify this aspect of his dramatic work as a compromise between comedy and tragedy, between "laughter and tears": "esa sonrisa que produce el teatro ligero, suave, optimista,"[2] lamenting the fact, in some cases, that despite his mastery of this genre he should not dedicate greater effort and time to the more serious drama for which he obviously has great talent.[3] But even with this reservation, based primarily on personal preference, none fails to concede this playwright's important contribution to the Spanish contemporary theater. One critic, commenting on the farce *El pobrecito embustero,* calls him "un gran comediógrafo,"[4] while yet another equally outstanding critic, referring to the dualism in Spanish contemporary drama between poetry and comedy ("el ensueño y el juego"), states that he is "Acaso el penetrante y hábil dramaturgo, de pleno siglo, que mejor ha abordado esta dualidad teatral..."[5]

While it is true that the major emphasis of Ruiz Iriarte's dramatic work is in the comic genre, a number of his outstanding dramatic works are in a more serious, transcendental vein, whether this be pure drama (*Los pájaros ciegos*, 1948; *Juanita va a Río de Janeiro*, 1948; and *Esta noche es la víspera*, 1958) or disguised, transcendental satire (*Un día en la gloria*, 1943, and *El gran minué*, 1950). This serious vein, as one critic points out, persists as an undercurrent of anguish even in those comedies which follow his special technical formula.[6] His

[1] Although Alejandro Casona has undoubtedly influenced the dramatic work of Ruiz Iriarte, the frequently-pointed-out similarity between Ruiz Iriarte's play *El puente de los suicidas*, Madrid, 1944, and Casona's *Prohibido suicidarse en primavera*, Mexico, 1937, is perhaps more superficial than real.

[2] Alfredo Marqueríe, *Veinte años de teatro en España* (Madrid: Editora Nacional, 1959), p. 169.

[3] Gonzalo Torrente Ballester, *Teatro español contemporáneo* (Madrid: Ediciones Guadarrama, 1957), p. 318.

[4] Federico Carlos Sainz de Robles, ed., "Prólogo," in *Teatro español 1952–1953* (Madrid: Edición Aguilar, S.A., 1954), p. 19.

[5] Angel Valbuena Prat, *Historia del teatro español* (Barcelona: Editorial Noguer, 1956), p. 665.

[6] Valbuena Prat, *Historia del teatro español*, pp. 665–66.

entire dramatic production, including the lighter genre, does, in fact, strive for a balance, a deliberate equilibrium between tragedy and comedy as the essence of reality—an ontological stand which can scarcely be considered an evasion or rejection of either extreme in favor of a lukewarm compromise with himself or with his public.

In this necessarily brief treatment of the Spanish dramatist's plays, the writer will endeavor to show how Ruiz Iriarte reconciles the element of anguish with comedy in some of his typical "comedias" and "farsas," beginning with an excellent example of this type of comedy: *Juego de niños.* A critical analysis of some of his satire and serious drama and a list of his plays will conclude this study.

JUEGO DE NIÑOS: A TYPICAL RUIZ IRIARTE "COMEDIA"

In *Juego de niños* (Madrid, 1952; "Premio Nacional de Teatro" 1952) Ruiz Iriarte achieves a perfect balance between drama and comedy by combining and reconciling a carefully disguised tragic concept of man's basic loneliness, insecurity, and need for affection with and within the structural elements of comedy and farce. Let us see how the author illustrates in this delightful comedy the ethical and aesthetic balance of his very personal dramatic formula from a conceptual, rather than purely technical standpoint.

The author himself states that *Juego de niños* "es una comedia optimista y desenvuelta, escrita con alegría y con afán."[7] From the beginning the comedy sparkles with the humor of its brilliant dialogue, its amusing and at times even farcical situations, and the light-hearted, youthful optimism of three very modern teenagers (Maité, Tony, and Manolín) who initiate and control the action of the play. The plot is quite simple. In order to oblige Ricardo, a middle-aged, attractive husband and the father of the two boys, to give up his interest in other women and return to his long-suffering, gentle wife Cándida, the young trio, with Maité the niece as the leader, engage the services of the girl's timid, idealistic French teacher, Marcelo, who is to pose as Cándida's fictitious lover. Since the "game" is to make the husband jealous, the sincere but in-

[7] "Autocrítica," in *Teatro español 1952–1953*, p. 223.

experienced teenagers joyfully pull the strings of their middle-aged marionettes and make things happen.

How do the marionettes react? Ricardo the husband, with his aggressiveness and boisterous self-assurance, has indeed a change of heart when faced with the possibility of losing the affection of his wife to a man whom he considers his inferior. But this "Don Juan" type, this would-be lady-killer, remains something of a caricature and his personality moves at all times within the realm of satire, comedy, and even farce. Marcelo and Cándida, on the other hand, are genuine, authentic personalities who, from the start, engage our full sympathy in spite of the fact that they are willing participants in the artificially conceived game of jealousy with its farcical situations. Yet it is not until the idealistic professor and the neglected wife betray their loneliness and desperate need for affection in the most moving and dramatically perfect scenes of the play, that the reader or audience becomes aware of the carefully disguised but definitely tragic undercurrent throughout.

The solution is in keeping with the author's concept of equilibrium: tragedy within comedy as a basis of life and reality. The dramatic problem is solved in a conventional, ethical manner. But the loneliness, especially for Marcelo, is left unresolved even though one might assume that he has enriched his spiritual life through his idealized love for Cándida. She, too, is aware of the tragedy of this loneliness when she tells her niece that one should never play—that is, "gamble"—with human affections, using hearts as forfeits. The so-called "juego de niños" had been, in fact, a most dangerous game, since the fiction created was in reality a poetic truth.

The "Authentic" Individual Within a Dramatic Formula in Comedies and Farces

This serious, semi-tragic note, this subtle undercurrent of man's anguished loneliness and his need for affection and recognition, disguised and all but lost in a cleverly contrived comedy structure and style, is always embodied in one or several characters (both main and secondary) of Ruiz Iriarte's "comedias" and even in his lighter farces.

The author creates different versions of a genuine or a"uthentic" individual[8] who has superior moral and spiritual qualities, but finds it difficult to adjust to a society with materialistic standards because of his or her idealism, excessive sensitivity, and lack of aggressiveness. Deprived of affection and appreciation, these "authentic" individuals are frequently victimized by their more fortunate, but far less authentic counterparts: the aggressive, worldly "Don Juan" type and the cold, scheming, vain or prudish woman. These two types are placed in contrast, and the author manages to reverse the value judgments of a vain, artificial society by showing that truth, virtue, and courage belong to the gentle, the timid, the sensitive, and at times, even to the so-called "social outcast."

An analysis of the author's conceptual dramatic formula, followed by some examples of these idealized, semi-tragic "authentic" protagonists in a few representative comedies and farces, should help bring into focus the manner in which this excellent playwright reconciles tragedy within comedy.[9]

A Dramatic Formula

Ruiz Iriarte's dramatic formula, based on man's loneliness, his need for affection, and his consequent withdrawal or escape into an inner, poetic reality or a make-believe, falsified reality of his own making may be summarized as follows:

(a) *The theme that controls all action is the need for love, the absence of which leads to anguished loneliness or insecurity.* For Ruiz Iriarte, the essence of life, as expressed through his characters, is happiness

[8] Ruiz Iriarte does not use the term "authentic" (*i.e.*, *auténtico*) to describe or define these types. Though reminiscent of the "authentic individual" concept defined in the philosophical "system" of the Spanish philosopher-critic José Ortega y Gasset (1883–1955), the similarity is limited to a partial definition of the Ortegan "authentic individual" as one who is true to his own "core of integrity" within his limited "circumstance." The term "authentic" is used here to refer to the protagonist who, after struggling, succeeds in being true to himself within his limited circumstance.

[9] For the sake of clarity and efficiency, and since the dramatic formula and plot analysis are interdependent, it is suggested that the summaries of the five comedies and farces following this section be read over once for identification of the protagonists discussed in the dramatic formula, then again more carefully for the application of the formula to each analysis.

through love, faith, and hope. But above all, love, for through love man can believe in God and fill his life with hope.[10] The theme and motivating factor in every play is the power of love and need of affection. This is true whether the individual represses that love (Marcelo, the idealistic professor in *Juego de niños*), is unaware of it and makes a false substitution (Paulina, the ambitious novelist in *Las mujeres decentes*), or rejects it because it comes too late (Lupe, the spinster in *La soltera rebelde*). The absence of love and appreciation leads to insecurity or anguished loneliness—the very essence of tragedy.[11]

(b) *In a society which generally values glamour, aggressiveness, and cleverness above virtue, sincerity, and honesty, the "authentic" individual cannot compete with his more favored counterpart and therefore suffers from the loneliness and rejection imposed by the vanity and selfishness of another or from false, inverted social standards.* Thus Cándida (*Juego de niños*) and Laura (*El café de las flores*) are betrayed by their insensitive husbands; Lorenzo, the scholar (*El pobrecito embustero*), and Andrés, the faithful husband (*El aprendiz de amante*), are rejected and ridiculed by their wives; marriage is being forced upon Lupe, a confirmed spinster (*La soltera rebelde*); Paulina, the ambitious novelist, is considered too virtuous and inexperienced to interest her public (*Las mujeres decentes*).

(c) *The rejected individual, seeking a solution to his loneliness, makes use of his imagination and either withdraws into his own inner poetic-intellectual reality, or fabricates a deception that will produce the desired happiness in terms of affection or appreciation or both.* Some of these authentic types, like Marcelo in *Juego de niños* or Esteban the organist in *La soltera rebelde*, have the spiritual strength to create an inner, poetic reality which is not merely a substitute for, but actually superior to an external, factual reality. This is an "authentic" use of their imagination, and while their dreams may not materialize, they remain true to themselves and to their ideals. But most of the protagonists in these comedies and farces try to attain a modicum of happiness by means

---

[10] Víctor Ruiz Iriarte, *La soltera rebelde* (Madrid: Ediciones ALFIL No. 37, 1952), p. 64.

[11] The concepts of love, anguished loneliness, and a superior poetic reality are of course reminiscent (though with a different aim and differently applied) of the Spanish poet-philosopher Miguel de Unamuno (1864–1936).

of a clever ruse—a fabricated deception. Thus Lorenzo, the ridiculed scholar, says that he is a dying man in order to gain affection and attention; Andrés, the virtuous lover, pretends at first that he *is* a Don Juan, a man who is fatally attractive to women, in order to win Catalina's love; and Paulina, the virtuous novelist, achieves her desired fame by assuming the role of a worldly woman with an unsavory reputation.

(d) *When happiness is achieved through a willful deception, it becomes falsified and the truly "authentic" individual, to regain his balance and self-respect, must eventually return and adjust to a reality, however difficult, that is at least in keeping with his own inner authenticity*. Thus Lupe the spinster, after trying to get rid of her "complex" doing violence to her true nature, gives up and goes back to her home town; Paulina the novelist exchanges the false glamour and fame she attained fraudulently for a more genuine happiness; Lorenzo the scholar finally admits that he is not going to die rather than hurt those he loves; and Andrés the virtuous husband prefers to lose his wife rather than continue in his role of a Don Juan. The problems of the betrayed wives Cándida and Laura are only partially solved since they both know that, regardless of their reconciliation, they cannot change the natures of their insensitive, egotistical husbands, and of course there always remains the truly unresolved loneliness of those who, like Marcelo, must be content to dream and remain in the periphery of life.

Application of the Dramatic Formula to Typical Comedies and Farces

Let us now illustrate and apply this serious dramatic formula to the plots of these typical comedies and farces from the standpoint of the protagonists:[12]

1. LAURA in *El café de las flores* (*Comedia en tres actos*, Madrid, 1953).

Laura, even more than Cándida, whom she greatly resembles, symbolizes the theme of anguished loneliness not only because her husband Gonzalo (who resembles Ricardo) has deserted her and she, too, must win him back, but especially because of the genuine compassion she feels for the loneliness of others. At the "Café de las

[12] For the sake of logic in the analysis the plays are not given here in chronological order.

flores," in the early hours of the morning, Laura meets and brings home an assortment of these lonely strangers, each with an unsolved problem, each seeking some form of escape from reality in order to make life more bearable. When Laura's husband returns home and finds among the guests the very woman with whom he was going to run away, Laura herself obliges him to conceal his identity so as not to hurt her rival, Marta, for whom she feels great compassion as her husband's innocent victim. As in the case of Ricardo and Cándida (*Juego de niños*) Gonzalo the husband realizes that he still loves his wife, and the marital problem is resolved. But the strangers, forced to leave their new-found dream world and refuge, find themselves once more outside in the harsh world of reality, alone and insecure.

2. LUPE in *La soltera rebelde* (*Comedia en tres actos*, Madrid, 1952).
Lupe, a confirmed spinster in her thirties, is being forced to marry against her will through the intervention of her sister Adelaida, a well-meaning, but frivolous and meddling society matron far more concerned with her social status than with her sister's genuine happiness. Lupe's excessive timidity toward men is explained to her by her young niece as a "freudian complex" obviously acquired when she was a child. So Lupe sets out on her own to destroy the "complex" by seeking the man who will not repel her when he kisses her. Yet even when she meets a kind, gentle, congenial soul like the organist Esteban she is unable to marry him because she knows that it is too late for her to love. Love, she feels, should be a part of one's youth. It cannot be set aside, for then it takes its own vengeance. So the spinster goes back to her home town, Montalbán, where she may find a quiet happiness more consistent with her authentic self.

3. LORENZO in *El pobrecito embustero* (*Farsa en tres actos*, Madrid, 1953).
Lorenzo the scholar is very much like Marcelo of *Juego de niños*. Although he is a learned and cultured scholar in a small provincial town, he is held in contempt and ridiculed by everyone—especially his ambitious, dissatisfied wife, Rosalía—because he is meek and unaggressive and hence a failure by their own materialistic, false standards. Desperately lonely and in need of affection and attention, he invents a lie, saying that he has an incurable disease and is a dying man. The deception works for a time and he fully enjoys the

attentions showered on him until, faced with the ethical dilemma of revealing the truth or hurting two sincere young people, he chooses the more ethical alternative, returning to his former "authentic" but unhappy status as a "sabio ridículo" and "pobre hombre." In the end his authenticity is rewarded when his wife, made aware of her own hypocrisy through an accidental circumstance, changes toward him and accepts him as he is.

4. ANDRÉS in *El aprendiz de amante* (*Farsa en tres actos*, Madrid, 1949).

Andrés is a gentle, idealistic, inexperienced young man who succeeds in marrying an attractive but frivolous young woman, Catalina, by creating the false impression that he is a dangerous Don Juan —the type of man she admires. When he confesses the truth to her on their wedding night, she rejects him, accusing him of marrying her through fraudulent means. In order to save her own "reputation" with her equally frivolous friends, she obliges him to persist in the deception, leading Madrid society to believe that he is actually an unprincipled rake, extremely dangerous to women. In spite of his wretchedness in this feigned and unsavory role, the deceit continues until another young woman, who has fallen in love with the genuinely virtuous, idealistic Andrés, makes the wife realize the true value of a husband capable of loyalty and devotion to one woman.

5. PAULINA in *Las mujeres decentes* (*Farsa en tres actos*, Madrid, 1949).

Paulina is the feminine version of both Andrés, the virtuous husband, and Lorenzo, the "embustero." She is an extremely proper but ambitious young woman whose novels are rejected because she lacks the false glamour demanded by the public. So she invents a love affair with a fictitious, dashing hero called Jerónimo—who really exists although she is unaware of him—and writes a best seller based on her feigned affair. Her rise to fame and fortune is immediate. The unsavory reputation created by the novel makes her the glamorous idol of the same public that had rejected her before. But like Andrés, the faithful lover, she cannot keep up pretenses. Her authenticity is finally restored by none other than the real Jerónimo who, unlike the dashing hero of her novel, is, like her, timid and virtuous.

Balance Between the Tragic and the Comic in Ruiz Iriarte's Comedies and Farces

How does Ruiz Iriarte reconcile the serious undercurrent of man's loneliness and his search for happiness with the comic and farcical aspects of his dramatic work? The answer seems to lie in his unusual ability to achieve a balance between the tragic and the comic by clothing the serious theme in comedy form and style.

In nearly every comedy and in some of his farces, the dramatic tensions created by the semi-tragic protagonist and the theme of loneliness threaten to explode, to come to the surface. There are moments of pain, of pathos, of tragic tension which are carefully though not obviously prepared. At such moments the play might easily turn into melodrama since there is no adequate preparation for a tragedy as such. But the author's impeccable taste, his excellent craftsmanship, his gentle sense of humor, and above all, his preference for balance and equilibrium come to the rescue. By means of an admittedly artificial device, an external incident, or an unexpected farcical situation, the play regains its balance between tears and laughter and the author achieves his aim, which is to bring forth a gentle smile from his audience—a smile of amusement combined with wisdom and compassion.

Ruiz Iriarte has many excellent comedy devices at his command. He is a skillful craftsman. Even in complicated plots and intrigues, the action develops rapidly and the dramatic conflict is resolved with a minimum of comic digressions, thus holding the interest of audience or reader to the end.

Some of the most characteristic elements of his comedy and farce are his humor, which is subtle and without bitterness, his gentle satire generally directed against the artificial facets of society with comical jabs at modern customs derived from American movies, his witty, sparkling dialogue even in serious situations, and the skillful use of traditional comedy tricks such as suspense, the surprise of the unexpected, farcical situations, and even slapstick. The most subtle part of his humor is revealed in his insight of human nature—its weaknesses and its strengths. He is particularly sensitive to feminine psychology and although he satirizes woman's frivolous, superficial nature at times, he does so with tongue in cheek and without malice.

On the other hand, he is quite critical of the aggressive, insensitive "Don Juan."

A characteristic device used by the author not only for comic effects but also as part of his dramatic technique in characterization, and perhaps as a partial answer to the artificiality of certain social values, is the frequent use of inverted value judgments of people, accepted customs, and social prejudices. Thus, the timid professor turns out to be the more genuine lover, and the children "educate" and pass judgment on their parents (*Juego de niños*); a wife frequently befriends and protects her husband's mistress (*Cuando ella es la otra* and *El café de las flores*); the worldly, frivolous type turns out to be a virtuous woman and vice versa (*La guerra empieza en Cuba*); the innocent young lady is the only dangerous menace to a confirmed bachelor's freedom (*Usted no es peligrosa*); a middle-aged, protected widow is in reality a "femme fatale" (*La vida privada de mamá*). In addition to these inverted value judgments, Ruiz Iriarte produces some very humorous effects by twisting and inverting certain statements in a totally unexpected and unconventional manner. An example of this is the amusing protest of a most experienced but "prudish" young lady who explains that she couldn't possibly run away with a married man without letting his wife know. And, sincerely shocked at such a thought she exclaims: "What would people think of me!" (*Cuando ella es la otra*).

Poetic Fantasy, Transcendental Satire, and Drama

Ruiz Iriarte has also written poetic and satirical plays based on fantasy, and some serious dramas.

In the combination of poetry and fantasy, *El landó de seis caballos*, produced in Madrid in 1950, is a masterpiece of intranscendental playfulness which the author himself recognizes as a "tour de force" constructed out of a simple event that took place years before the action. Yet it has extraordinary charm and a poignant symbolism. In one and the same environment, the author "plays" with two worlds of reality and two categories of people: the concrete reality with its rational, "normal" people, and the world of fantasy with those who have lost contact with the factual world. As the intrigue develops, the world of make-believe becomes more genuine and more desirable than the other. The situation is as follows:

Five young people, two men and three women, all strangers to each other, are summoned with an identical written invitation from an unknown *Duque* to his old, neglected mansion in an isolated part of the woods near the city of Ávila. He promises in the note that if they accept the invitation they may find the happiness they have been searching for by spending one evening there. But when they arrive, they discover that the house is in the hands of four elderly people: an old lady, Doña Adelita, and three old men. The *Duque* is nowhere to be found. The elderly people seem to be quite out of their minds, since they insist on creating a make-believe world, converting a sofa into a beautiful carriage drawn by six horses, taking rides in the parks of Madrid while actually remaining in the living room, meeting and talking to royalty and other persons long since dead, and dressing up in the style of some forty years ago. By creating their own dream world they have managed to make time stand still so that they may continue to live in the early years of the twentieth century—their golden age. Like children, they play at make-believe and are supremely happy.

The contrast between these "irrational" old people and the "rational" modern young people who have come to this mansion in search of happiness within the realm of a concrete reality—love, marriage, or money—is the basis of this delightful and absurd farce. The explanation of the mystery comes at the end, but it is significant only in the light that it throws on the main theme of the farce—one which is far from farcical: Each person seeks happiness but not everyone has the imagination to create beauty and happiness where it does not exist. Doña Adelita, the little old lady, had solved a tragic problem for her companions by simply converting life into a game. Since dreams are a game, life too can be a game. And Isabel, one of the rational young ladies who is fortunately endowed with sensitivity and imagination, voices the same idea when she says to the equally sensitive archaeologist that life is truly beautiful when it is a dream. The symbolism of the title becomes clear when she adds that perhaps happiness is nothing more than taking rides in a nonexistent carriage drawn by six horses.

In both *Un día en la gloria* and *El gran minué*, Ruiz Iriarte reveals a skillful mastery of transcendental satire disguised in poetic fantasy.

Un día en la gloria, produced in 1943, was the author's first dramatic work. It brought him immediate recognition as a dramatist of genuine talent and promise. This one-act farce is in reality a transcendental satire, an allegorical fantasy of an imaginary world ("la gloria") where those who have achieved fame through public opinion reside and walk about as the shadows of man's memories.

The satire is directed against the twentieth-century values which relegate to oblivion the truly great in history, in art, in literature, while raising to fame the modern, artificial idols of a materialistic civilization: movie actors, boxers, chorus girls, and thieves. Only the great Sarah Bernhardt, who walks among the shadows of the great, has faith that some day the poets, the musicians, and the artists will again ascend the steps of fame. The allegorical farce ends with the departure of Napoleon from the world of glory since he knows that public opinion has replaced him with an image of the movie idol who portrayed him.

But it is in *El gran minué*, one of Ruiz Iriarte's most beautiful plays, produced in 1950, where a transcendental satire of political intrigue and human weaknesses is most perfectly combined with the poetic-fantasy medium of a delightful "ballet-farce." *El gran minué* is a farce full of irony and satire of universal significance in which the characters, as the author himself points out in his "autocrítica," move about like the dolls of a music box. The time is the eighteenth century and the theme might be summarized as a dialogue or verbal duel between Valentín—the young, inexperienced, enthusiastic, and idealistic country lad who believes that he can reform the corrupted court of civilization by introducing his poetic concepts of virtue and morality—and Valentín's arch-enemy, Gravelot—the old and powerful minister of the court, who has learned through experience to be a cynic and a philosopher, or as he calls himself, an indifferent intellectual. Thus the poetry of inexperienced youth opposes the philosophy of experienced old age; youthful idealism crosses swords with cynical intellectualism. It is not until Valentín runs away with the king's favorite, the youthful, innocent Diana, and learns the meaning of love that he gains the necessary wisdom to understand human nature as an inevitable mixture of good and evil. Gravelot the cynic significantly remarks that on that morning Valentín the poet died and Valentín the philosopher was born.

The critic Alfredo Marqueríe includes *Esta noche es la víspera* (*Comedia*[13] *en un prologo y dos actos*, Madrid, 1958) as one of the three full-scale, outstanding plays written by Ruiz Iriarte, in which the author "se adentró más que por los vericuetos, por los caminos reales del teatro."[14] The author himself classifies this work as one of the most difficult plays he has ever written because of the limitations imposed in maintaining two hours of sustained dramatic tension by both the theme and the static situation. The success of the play and the excellent reviews it received from the critics are ample proof of Ruiz Iriarte's talent as a writer of serious drama—a talent which he had already revealed in such plays as *Los párajos ciegos* (produced in 1948) and in the short but almost painfully tragic dialogue called *Juanita va a Río de Janeiro*, written for a private performance some time before its 1948 publication.

The situation in *Esta noche es la víspera*, which is a flashback from the Prologue, reveals the tensions, fears, and anxieties of a number of passengers who are obliged to take refuge during the night in a deserted cabin when their plane, bound for Paris, is grounded by a snowstorm. Each passenger, desperately anxious to reach his destination, resents the delay decreed by Fate. A young woman who is leaving her invalid husband for another man, a widow who wants the freedom which Paris can give her, a writer who is willing to find happiness at the expense of another, a disillusioned woman who wants vengeance, a young married couple on their honeymoon, a girl running away from home, a poor devil who always feels rejected by others, a man who intends to commit a crime in Paris which he doesn't actually want to carry out—each of these men and women (excepting a young priest) is driven by hatred, ambition, or arrogance to commit a crime against his fellow man or against himself. Fate in the guise of a storm has offered them all a reprieve so that each

---

[13] It should be remembered that "comedia" in Spanish is a much broader term than the English word "comedy" since "comedia" may also refer to serious drama. *Esta noche es la víspera* is not a "comedy" in any sense of the word.

[14] Marqueríe, *Veinte años de teatro en España*, p. 176.

may look into his heart and make a choice based on free will. When the pilot finally calls those passengers who wish to continue their trip to Paris, each one has found the solution to his preconceived crime and turns back, making a choice based on a truth each had deliberately hidden from himself.

The play does not end as a "tragedy" in the dramatic sense of the word. But is not "tragedy" implicit in man's spiritual blindness and the very fact that, but for the intervention of Fate, man may be driven by his uncontrolled passions and inherent weaknesses?

Ruiz Iriarte does not generally write tragedy or drama as such and most of his work admittedly falls in the category of comedy and farce. But despite his insistence on the theatre as a means of amusement and joy, and despite his clever technical devices and elements of humor in comedy or farce, satire, or poetic fantasy, the tragic undercurrent which runs throughout his dramatic work renders meaningless any attempt to classify him as an intranscendental playwright.

Ruiz Iriarte does not evade the tragic truth of man's anguished loneliness. He merely disguises it and finds a possible solution for it in a "poetic reality" to which all men have access provided they have the imagination and sensitivity to convert—not pervert—their own harsh, external reality into an inner, poetic one. We have the right to dream, but not to escape into that dream and thereby lose touch with our own reality, for in doing so we may lose our most precious possession: our personal, individual authenticity.

In the opinion of this writer, the master craftsman of comic form disguises deliberately and perhaps too well a playwright of great depth and potentially tragic content.

I.M.S.

List of Plays by Ruiz Iriarte

Un día en la gloria (Farsa en un acto) Estrenos: Zaragoza, 1943; Madrid, 1944. Ediciones: en "Colección Teatro" ALFIL No. 35 (Extra).

El puente de los suicidas (Comedia en tres actos) Madrid, 1944.

Don Juan se ha puesto triste (Comedia en tres actos) Madrid, 1945.

Academia de amor (Comedia en tres actos) "Premio Piquer," 1946; Madrid, 1946.

El cielo está cerca (Comedia en tres actos) Madrid, 1947.

La señora, sus ángeles y el diablo (Comedia en tres actos) Madrid, 1947.

El aprendiz de amante (Farsa en tres actos) Valencia, 1947; Madrid, 1949. ALFIL No. 35 (Extra).

Los pájaros ciegos (Comedia dramática en tres actos) Madrid, 1948.

Juanita va a Río de Janeiro (Diálogo dramático) Madrid, 1948. ALFIL No. 100 (Extra: Antología).

Las mujeres decentes (Farsa en tres actos) Barcelona y Madrid, 1949. ALFIL No. 5 (Extra).

El landó de seis caballos (Farsa en dos actos) Madrid, 1950. ALFIL No. 80 (Extra); en *Teatro español 1949–1950*, ed. F. C. Sainz de Robles (Madrid: Edición Aguilar, 1951).

El gran minué (Farsa-ballet en un prólogo y tres actos) Madrid, 1950. ALFIL No. 5 (Extra); en *Teatro español 1950–1951*.

Cuando ella es la otra (Farsa en tres actos) Barcelona, 1951; Madrid, 1952. ALFIL No. 17.

Juego de niños (Comedia en tres actos) "Premio Nacional de Teatro," 1952; Madrid, 1952. ALFIL No. 8, en *Teatro español 1951–1952*.

La soltera rebelde (Comedia en tres actos) Madrid, 1952. ALFIL No. 37.

El pobrecito embustero (Farsa en tres actos) Madrid, 1953. ALFIL No. 80 (Extra); en *Teatro español 1952–1953*.

El café de las flores (Comedia en tres actos) Madrid, 1953. ALFIL No. 86.

La cena de los tres reyes (Farsa en tres actos) Madrid, 1954. ALFIL No. 111.

Usted no es peligrosa (Comedia en tres actos) Madrid, 1954. ALFIL No. 118.

La guerra empieza en Cuba (Farsa en dos actos) Madrid, 1955. ALFIL No. 142; en *Teatro español 1955–1956*.

La vida privada de mamá (Comedia en dos actos) Madrid, 1956. ALFIL No. 168.

También la buena gente (Farsa en dos actos) Barcelona, 1957.

Esta noche es la víspera (Comedia en un prólogo y dos actos) Madrid, 1958. ALFIL No. 218; en *Teatro español 1958–1959*.

Una investigación privada (Farsa en dos actos) Madrid, 1958.

Tengo un millón (Comedia en dos actos) Madrid, 1960. ALFIL No. 288.

De París viene mamá (Farsa en dos actos) Madrid, 1960.

JUEGO DE NIÑOS

"Juego de niños" literally means "A Children's Game." A more appropriate title in English would be "A Dangerous Game."

REPARTO

PERSONAJES	ACTORES
CÁNDIDA	Tina Gascó
MAITÉ	Victoria Rodríguez
MANOLITA........................	Antonia Mas
ROSITA	Rosa Lacasa
RICARDO	Juan Cortés
MARCELO	Carlos Casaravilla
TONY	Manuel Alejandre
MANOLÍN	Carlos Sánchez

Esta obra se estrenó en Madrid, el 8 de enero de 1952 en el Teatro Reina Victoria

Acto Primero

Nos hallamos, durante el transcurso de estos tres actos, en la estancia más íntima y más familiar del piso que la familia Del Valle habita en el barrio de Salamanca. Es una magnífica casa, construída recientemente, en la zona que se comprende entre Velázquez y Serrano. La vivienda no es muy grande, desde luego, pero sí es lujosa— 5
de un lujo alegre—y extraordinariamente cómoda. Tiene garaje en el patio, nevera en la cocina, dos cuartos de baño y aire frío y caliente. La habitación que se representa en escena es como un resumen de la vida familiar de los Del Valle ...

Después de tan explícitas acotaciones casi resulta obvio, cierta- 10
mente, anotar la estructura de la pieza y lo que contiene. Buena parte del fondo lo ocupa una cristalera que separa este interior de una pequeña terraza de esas a las que, por fortuna, son tan aficionados los arquitectos contemporáneos. En la terraza, el toldo está echado y hay algunas plantas verdes bajo el antepecho. Al fondo, también 15
hacia la derecha, una entrada que seguramente conduce al vestíbulo. Puertas, a la derecha y a la izquierda. En el centro del salón, frente al público, un gran sofá con sillones. Hacia la izquierda, una mesa redonda con varias sillas en torno. Algún cuadro de excelente escuela moderna. Son, aproximadamente, las nueve y media de una mañana 20
de primavera. Sol en la terraza y luz radiante en el interior.

Al levantarse el telón,[1] ROSITA, la doncella, con un gran plumero en la mano, termina de hacer la limpieza de la estancia. En seguida se oye la voz de MANOLÍN que entra, muy alborozado. Este MANOLÍN es un impetuoso ciudadano de unos quince o dieciséis años. Viste 25

[1] *Al levantarse el telón* As the curtain rises

pijama. Trae toda la cara enjabonada[2] y una brocha de afeitar en la mano.

MANOLÍN

¡Papá! ¡Mamá!

ROSITA

¡Chist! ¡Silencio, señorito Manolín! ¿Qué significan esas voces?[3]
5 Su papá y su mamá todavía no han salido de su habitación...

MANOLÍN (*Muy ufano*)

¿Te das cuenta? ¿Eh? ¿Te das cuenta, Rosita?

ROSITA

¿De qué tengo que darme cuenta?

MANOLÍN

¿Te das cuenta de que me estoy afeitando?

ROSITA

¡Ah, bueno!

MANOLÍN (*Indignado*)

10 ¿Cómo que ah, bueno?[4] ¡Si me afeito es porque ya me ha salido la barba![5]

ROSITA

¡Quia!

---

[2] *Trae toda la cara enjabonada* His whole face is covered with soap
[3] *¿Qué significan esas voces?* What do you mean by shouting so?
[4] *¿Cómo ... bueno?* What do you mean, "Oh, come now!"
[5] *¡ya me ha salido la barba!* I have to start shaving now! (*literally*, I've started growing a beard!)

MANOLÍN

¡Rosita, no seas flamenca!

ROSITA (*Un suspiro*)

No tiene usted ninguna barba, señorito Manolín. Lo que pasa es que tampoco tiene usted paciencia para esperar a que le salga, y claro, se afeita usted sin más ni más ... Pero lo que es barba, ya, ya.[6]

MANOLÍN (*Con furia*)

¡Te digo que me está saliendo la barba! ¡Porras! 5

(*Entra* TONY. *Es otro muchacho algo mayor que Manolín. Un par de años, quizá. Acaba de levantarse de la cama; pijama, zapatillas y bata. Con la toalla al cuello, pasa camino del cuarto de baño.*)

TONY

¡Rosita! ¿Tú sabes si están planchados mis pantalones blancos de tenis? 10

ROSITA

No, señorito Tony.

TONY

Entonces, no te digo nada.[7] Pero a las doce tengo que estar en la Universitaria, y de punta en blanco. ¿Me oyes, rica?

MANOLÍN

Hombre; lo que no sé es por qué siempre que te diriges a Rosita la has de llamar rica ... 15

TONY

Porque lo es. (*Cariñosísimo*) Porque es muy rica. Porque es riquísima ... ¿Verdad, guapa?

---

[6] *Pero ... ya, ya* But as far as having to shave ... now, really!
[7] *Entonces, no te digo nada* Well, I don't mean to insist

ROSITA (*Huyendo*)

Estése usted quieto, señorito Tony.

MANOLÍN

Si te aprovechas de Rosita en mi presencia, se lo digo a mamá ...[8]

TONY

Anda, si está aquí el chivato.[9]

MANOLÍN (*Furioso*)

¡No me llames chivato!

TONY

5 ¡Huy! Adiós, pequeño.

MANOLÍN

¡No me llames pequeño! ¿No te das cuenta de que me estoy afeitando?

TONY

Ya, ya. Las ganas ...

MANOLÍN (*Ofendidísimo*)

¡Tony!

TONY

10 Pero, chico, ¿por qué tienes esas prisas por ser mayor?[10] Si tú supieras las responsabilidades que adquiere uno cuando se hace hombre ... (*Y se va silbando alegremente, sin el menor sentido de la responsabilidad, por supuesto.*)

[8] *se lo digo a mamá* I'll tell mother (Note that *digo* here means future)
[9] *Anda, si está aquí el chivato* Well! So the kid brother is here
[10] *¿por qué ... mayor?* why are you in such a hurry to grow up?

MANOLÍN

Lo que presume este idiota ... Y todo porque tiene dos años más que yo.

ROSITA (*Riendo*)

¡Pobre señorito Manolín!

(*Entra, como una tromba,* MAITÉ. *Es una adorable adolescente. Viste flamantes pantalones. Trae en la mano un vestido de su pertenencia.*)

MAITÉ

Buenos días, primo.

MANOLÍN (*Gruñendo*)

Buenos días ...

MAITÉ

¡Rosita! Encanto, cielo mío ...

ROSITA

¡Huy!

MAITÉ

Mira, preciosa. Necesito que para esta noche me planches y me requeteplanches este traje con toda esa gracia que Dios te ha dado ... ¿Lo harás?

ROSITA

¡Qué remedio!

MAITÉ

Gracias, tesoro. ¡Huy! ¡Lo que te quiero! Dame un beso... (*Confidencial*) Estoy invitada a la puesta de largo de Juanita Lara.[11] Es

[11] *la puesta ... Lara* Juanita Lara's coming out party (from *ponerse de largo* to wear long, *i.e.*, "grown up" clothes)

una familia muy graciosa, ¿sabes? Millonarios. Pero de esta clase de millonarios que te los quedas mirando y, sin saber por qué, eso de tener millones te parece una ordinariez ...[12]

(MANOLÍN, *que lleva un rato paseando en torno a su prima para hacerse notar, se acerca al fin poseído de cierta esperanza.*)

MANOLÍN

Oye, primita, ¿te has fijado? Ya me afeito ...

MAITÉ (*Muy superior*)

Vamos, anda, niño.

MANOLÍN

¡Maité!

MAITÉ

No seas fantástico. Y no me entretengas, que va a llegar el profesor de francés y luego tengo que ir a la peluquería ... (*Y sale alegrísima, tarareando, muy feliz, una canción del día.* MANOLÍN, *como un energúmeno, comienza a darle puntapiés al mueble que tiene más cerca.*)

MANOLÍN

¡Maldita sea! Le voy a dar a uno una patada ...[13]

ROSITA

!Señorito!

MANOLÍN

Ríete tú; eso es. Después de que la culpa de todo es tuya ...[14]

---

[12] *eso ... ordinariez* their having millions seems just plain vulgar
[13] *Le voy a dar ... patada* I'm going to kick someone
[14] *Después ... es tuya* After all, *you're* to blame for everything

ROSITA

¿Qué está usted diciendo?

MANOLÍN

Tuya y de nadie más. ¿No me dijiste el otro día que para besarte a ti había de tener barba?

ROSITA (*Ríe más*)

Pero, señorito ... ¡Ay Dios mío, qué chiquillo!

MANOLÍN

Ríete, ríete. Así sois las mujeres.[15] ¡Maldita sea! 5

(*Sale* MANOLÍN, *francamente herido.* ROSITA *aún ríe y continúa su tarea. Una pausa levísima. Por el fondo, con grandes precauciones, asoma* RICARDO. *Es un hombre de algunos más de cuarenta años, mundano y simpático, de magnífico aspecto, un poco marchito en estos momentos. Trae el sombrero puesto y la gabardina al brazo.*) 10

RICARDO

¡Chist! ¡Rosita!

ROSITA (*Sofocando un grito*)

¡Ay! ¡El señor!

RICARDO

El mismo, hija. Pero no grites.

ROSITA

Pero, ¿es que no ha dormido el señor en casa?

RICARDO

Tú verás. 15

ROSITA

¡Otra vez!

[15] *Así sois las mujeres* You women are all alike

RICARDO

Sí, hija. No sé qué me pasa, pero siempre que ceno fuera de casa se me hace tardísimo...[16] Y ya ves tú. Es una fatalidad. (*Transición*) Oye... Mi mujer y mis hijos, ¿duermen todavía?

ROSITA

No, señor. Los señoritos ya se han levantado. Y la sobrina del señor, 5 también.

RICARDO

¡Caramba! (*Muy molesto*) Pero, ¿por qué se madruga tanto en esta casa?

ROSITA

Son las diez de la mañana, señor.

RICARDO

¿De veras? ¿Las diez? ¡Qué barbaridad! Hay que ver cómo pasa el 10 tiempo.[17] Y mira tú. Mi reloj tiene las dos. Pero las dos de la madrugada, ¿comprendes? Y, claro, como siempre que miraba el reloj eran las dos, cuando se ha hecho de día, no me lo quería creer ... Pensé que era una broma.

ROSITA

Ya, ya. (*Sonríe*) Es lo que pasa siempre.

RICARDO

15 Mira, Rosita. Necesito entrar en mi cuarto sin que se enteren los muchachos. Tú ya los conoces. Mis hijos y mi sobrina no me tienen ningún respeto, y en estas ocasiones abusan ... Si se enteran de que no he pasado la noche en casa, estoy perdido. Después, si es preciso, ya inventaré algo ... (*Muy satisfecho con el hallazgo*) ¡Diré lo del reloj!

[16] *se me hace tardísimo* I lose track of time (*literally*, it becomes very late for me)
[17] *Hay que ver ... tiempo* How time does fly

ROSITA

¡No! Lo del reloj, no.

RICARDO

¿No?

ROSITA

No, señor. Venga el señor ... Sígame. De puntillas. Sin ruido. No, lo mejor será que el señor se quite los zapatos. Es un truco que aprendí en la última casa que estuve. 5

RICARDO

¡Hola! ¿Se descalzaba el señor?

ROSITA

¡Ca! Era la señora.

RICARDO

¡Caray! Pero qué falta de moral tiene la gente ... (RICARDO, *que se ha descalzado apresuradamente, ahora, en pie, con los zapatos en la mano, se dispone a marchar tras de* ROSITA.) ¡Qué buena eres, Rosita! (*Todo* 10 *gratitud*) ¡Y qué bonita! Oye, ¿sabes que estas primeras horas de la mañana te sientan muy bien?

ROSITA

Pero, ¿es que me va a piropear el señor?[18]

RICARDO (*Con un suspiro*)

Perdona, mujer. Es que no lo puedo remediar ...

(*Con su última frase ha salido* ROSITA. *Cuando* RICARDO *va a seguirla,* 15 *de puntillas y con los zapatos en la mano, en otra puerta aparecen* MANOLÍN *y* TONY. RICARDO, *al oirlos, se queda inmóvil y aterrado.*)

[18] *¿es que ... el señor?* are you trying to flatter me, sir?

TONY

¡Papá!

MANOLÍN

¡Mi padre!

RICARDO

Sí, hijo. Tu padre ...

MANOLÍN

¿A dónde vas, papá? ¿Se puede saber qué haces con el sombrero
5 puesto y los zapatos en la mano?

RICARDO

¡Je! (*Azaradísimo*) Tienes razón, hijo. La costumbre es, precisamente, lo contrario. El sombrero en la mano y los zapatos en la cabeza ...

MANOLÍN

¿Qué estás diciendo, papá?

RICARDO (*Más azarado aún*)

¡Je! Nada. No digo nada ... (*Amabilísimo*) ¿Comó estáis, hijos?
10 ¿Estáis bien?

TONY

Nosotros muy bien, papá. ¿Y tú?

RICARDO

Pues, ¿qué quieres que te diga, Tony? A estas horas está uno molido ...[19] (RICARDO *se ha sentado en el sofá y, desesperadamente, se da aire con el sombrero. Los dos muchachos, en pie, se han situado uno a cada lado*
15 *de su padre y, desde hace un rato, lo examinan con una impresionante actitud fiscal.*)[20]

[19] *Pues, ... está uno molido* Well, what can I say, Tony? At this early hour I'm completely worn out

[20] *desde ... actitud fiscal* they have been watching him for some time as if they were stern prosecutors

TONY

¡Manolín! Tengo una sospecha. Me parece que papá no ha dormido esta noche en casa ...

MANOLÍN

¡Sopla!

RICARDO (*Muy digno*)

Manolín, no seas ordinario. (*Los dos chicos hablan dirigiéndose el uno al otro, como si estuvieran solos.* RICARDO *los mira alternativamente con mucho susto.*) 5

MANOLÍN

Pero si ya hacía tiempo que no teníamos que regañarle ...[21]

TONY

Pues ya ves. Está visto que a los padres no se les puede dar alas ...[22]

RICARDO (*Dolorosamente*)

Tony, Manolín. Yo os explicaré lo ocurrido ...

MANOLÍN (*Severísimo*)

¡Papá! 10

RICARDO

¿Qué?

MANOLÍN

Dicen las estadísticas que el noventa por ciento de los padres de familia que desaparecen durante la noche, por la mañana no pueden explicar dónde han estado. Hay un diez por ciento que lo explican todo. Pero es mentira.[23] Tú eres de ese diez por ciento, papá ... 15

[21] *Pero si ... regañarle* Why, we hadn't had to scold him for quite some time now

[22] *Está visto ... dar alas* It's obvious that one can't give parents too much freedom (wings)

[23] *Pero es mentira* But what they say is a lie (*i.e.*, the ten per cent who explain it all are lying)

RICARDO

¡Manolín!

MANOLÍN (*Escapando*)

¡Ay!

(*Irrumpe en escena* MAITÉ. *Se lanza a los brazos de* RICARDO *y le besa y le abraza con mucho mimo.*)

MAITÉ

5 ¡Tío Ricardo!

RICARDO

¡Querida sobrina!

MAITÉ

Ya sé que no has dormido esta noche en casa ... ¡No! ¡No te disculpes! Es tu destino. Tu padeces un complejo de atracción femenina.

RICARDO (*Desconfiado*)

10 ¿Qué quiere decir eso, Maité?

MAITÉ

¡Que te gustan todas!

RICARDO

¿De veras crees que eso es un complejo?

MAITÉ

¡Huy! Menudo. Pero tú no eres el responsable. La culpa es de ellas ...

RICARDO

Si vieras, hija, que eso lo he pensado yo muchas veces.[24] (*Transición. Muy apesadumbrado*) Pero esta vez os equivocáis. No hay ninguna mujer. No negaré que en otras ocasiones ... Pero desde hace bastante tiempo soy otro hombre. Sí, otro hombre, ni más ni menos. Lo de esta noche ... (*Transición*) ¿Es necesario que os explique las causas que esta noche me han obligado a no dormir en casa? 5

LOS TRES MUCHACHOS (*Al tiempo*)

¡Sí!

RICARDO (*Con dignísima amargura*)

¿No basta mi palabra?

LOS TRES MUCHACHOS

¡No!

MAITÉ

¡Ay, qué granuja! 10

RICARDO

Muy bien. Pues oíd. (*Baja los ojos.*) Esta noche he sido víctima de la fatalidad ...

MANOLÍN

¡Pobre!

RICARDO (*Indignado*)

¡Manolín! ¡Si no te callas, te doy un sopapo![25]

MANOLÍN

¡Ay! 15

---

[24] *Si vieras ... veces* You know, my child, I've often thought so too
[25] ¡*Si no ... un sopapo*! If you don't keep quiet, I'll slap you!

MAITÉ

Bueno. Pero, ¿dónde has pasado la noche?

RICARDO (*Con solemnidad*)

¡En Ávila! (*Los tres chicos hacen un unámine movimiento de protesta.*)

LOS TRES MUCHACHOS

¡No!

MANOLÍN (*Muy cargado*)

Hombre, no. ¡En Ávila, no!

RICARDO

5 ¿Es que no os gusta Ávila?

TONY

No es eso, papá. Lo que nos asombra es tu falta de imaginación. El verano pasado te escapaste tres días y a la vuelta nos dijiste que venías de Pamplona ...

MANOLÍN

Es que, para despistar, siempre escoge ciudades muy de derechas ...

MAITÉ (*Divertidísima*)

10 ¡Ay, qué embustero!

RICARDO

¡Maité! ¿Embustero tu tío?

MAITÉ

¡Sí! Embustero, embustero, embustero ...

RICARDO

Pero, ¿es que no vais a creerme?

MANOLÍN

¡Ni pizca!

RICARDO (*Desesperado*)

¡Oh!

(*Aparece* ROSITA *en el fondo.*)

ROSITA

¡Chiss! La señora ... (*Los tres chicos, al oirla, se alborotan, muy inquietos.*)

LOS TRES MUCHACHOS

¡Oh! 5

ROSITA

La señora viene hacia aquí, y si se entera de que los señoritos están riñendo al señor, ya van listos los señoritos ...[26] (ROSITA *se marcha por donde entró.*)

TONY

¡Sálvese el que pueda![27]

MAITÉ

¡Ay, tío! ¡Qué suerte tienes! 10

TONY

Mamá tiene la culpa de que papá esté tan mal criado. Siempre que le estamos amonestando aparece ella para defenderle ...

MANOLÍN

Y que lo digas.[28] Así no se puede educar a un padre ...

(MAITÉ, TONY, y MANOLÍN, *juntos, salen muy aprisa. Entra* CÁNDIDA. *Es una mujer joven todavía. Tiene una noble belleza natural que el tiempo* 15 *y la maternidad no han disminuído. Es sencilla, muy sencilla, pero quizá entre muchas se la distinguiría al instante. Se dirige a* RICARDO *muy natural y muy afectuosa.*)

[26] *ya ... los señoritos* you young people had better watch out
[27] ¡*Sálvese el que pueda*! Everyone on his own!
[28] *Y que lo digas* You can say *that* again!

CÁNDIDA

¡Ricardo! ¿Cómo estás, querido?

RICARDO

¡Je! Buenos días, Cándida. ¿Has descansado?

CÁNDIDA

Yo, muy bien. ¿Y tú?

RICARDO

Nada. Estoy rendido.

CÁNDIDA

5 Se ve. Tienes una cara espantosa. ¡Pobrecito mío! (*Le besa amorosamente.*) Dime la verdad, Ricardo. ¿Te han molestado los chicos?

RICARDO

¡Oh, no!

CÁNDIDA

¿Te han faltado al respeto?

RICARDO

Bueno ... Un poco. ¡Je! Lo de siempre.

CÁNDIDA

10 ¡Ay, ay, Dios mío! ¡Qué cosas te habrán dicho![29] Mira, Ricardo, yo estoy asustada con estos muchachos. Son incorregibles. Dicen y hacen verdaderas barbaridades.[30] Claro que la culpa es tuya. ¡No sabes ser padre! ¡Eso es todo![31] Juegas a las cartas con Tony y os

[29] ¡*Qué cosas te habrán dicho*! What dreadful things they must have said to you!
[30] *Dicen ... barbaridades* They say and do the most atrocious things
[31] ¡*No sabes ... todo*! You don't know how to act like a father! That's all there is to it!

hacéis trampas el uno al otro. Te pones a boxear con Manolín y hay que ver el pequeño cómo se aprovecha y las palizas que te da. Y, por si fuera poco todo eso,[32] te hacen muchísima gracia los modernismos de mi sobrina, que a mí me producen escalofríos. Yo no sé dónde ha aprendido esa chica todo lo que sabe. Cuando termine sus estudios 5 y la devolvamos a su casa no sé lo que va a pensar de nosotros y de Madrid su madre, mi pobre hermana, tan anticuada y tan apegada a su provincia ... (*Transición*) ¡Mi pobre Ricardo! ¡Debes estar cansadísimo! ¿Quieres una taza de café? ¿O un poco de té? ¿Qué prefieres? (*Surge* ROSITA *como antes*) 10

ROSITA

No se moleste más la señora.[33] Los señoritos ya no están escuchando ...

CÁNDIDA

¡Ah! Gracias, Rosita. (*Sale* ROSITA. CÁNDIDA *se ha transformado. Es otra mujer. Su sonrisa, solícita y amorosa, se cambia por un mohín de superior desdén. Cuando habla, al cabo del silencio, en su voz hay un eco de contenida irritación.*) ¿Quieres ponerte esos zapatos? Estás francamente 15 cómico ... Y no sé si debo reir o llorar. (RICARDO, *muy mohino, se sienta en el sofá y comienza a ponerse los zapatos.*)

RICARDO

Nunca comprenderé por qué, en estas circunstancias, siempre haces la misma comedia ...

CÁNDIDA

Porque no quiero que Manolín y Tony me compadezcan. Prefiero 20 que vean en mí una insensata que te lo perdona todo y te mima, antes que una pobre mujer que sufre y llora en silencio cuando no la ve nadie ... Tengo esa soberbia. No podría soportar que mis hijos tuvieran lástima de mí. (*Un silencio*)

---

[32] *Y, por si ... eso* And to make matters worse (*i.e.*, as if that weren't enough)

[33] *No se moleste más la señora* Madam doesn't have to trouble herself any longer (*i.e.*, she doesn't have to pretend any longer)

RICARDO

Cándida.

CÁNDIDA

¿Qué?

RICARDO

Yo quiero darte una explicación.

CÁNDIDA (*Con suave ironía*)

¿A mí también vas a contarme lo de Ávila?

RICARDO

5 ¡Je! ¿Me has oído?

CÁNDIDA

Todo.

RICARDO

Entonces, no. No te contaré lo de Ávila.

CÁNDIDA (*Suave*)

¡Gracias!

RICARDO

Bueno ... , quiero decir que a ti te diré la verdad.

CÁNDIDA

10 ¡Otra mentira!

RICARDO (*Muy ofendido*)

Pero, mujer ... ¿Es que no crees en mi palabra?

CÁNDIDA

Nada.

RICARDO

¡Es el colmo! En esta casa nadie cree en mi palabra. Ni mi mujer. Ni mis hijos, ni mi sobrina. ¡Soy un desgraciado!

CÁNDIDA (*Sonriendo*)

Ricardo, por Dios, no seas farsante. Para ti la verdad siempre es otra mentira. Muchísimo más graciosa que la primera: eso, sí. Pero, esta vez, cállatela. Te aseguro que no tengo ninguna curiosidad por saber 5 dónde has pasado la noche ... (*Un silencio. De pronto,* RICARDO *la mira. Se vuelve hacia ella, sincero, apasionado.*)

RICARDO

¡Cándida!

CÁNDIDA

¡Ay! ¡Me has asustado!

RICARDO

¡Tú sabes que te quiero! 10

CÁNDIDA (*Le mira y sonríe*)

Me quieres de un modo muy curioso. Me quieres cuando vuelves de la aventura con otras mujeres. Me quieres cuando regresas a casa, después de toda una noche de ausencia.[34] Me quieres siempre a la vuelta de algo. ¿No crees que ese cariño resulta un poco egoísta, Ricardo? ¿Piensas que puedo sentirme muy orgullosa? ¡Oh! Ya sé 15 que soy para ti el reposo, la paz, la convalecencia ... Todo eso tan bonito. Y tan triste, tan triste. Quizá tú no tienes la culpa. Quizá a los veinte años de matrimonio, éste es el único amor posible ... (*Bruscamente, en un arrebato apasionado que rompe la serenidad de las palabras anteriores*)[35] ¡Pero si tú supieras cómo envidio a las otras! Las 20 envidio tanto como las odio ...

[34] *después ... ausencia* after being out all night
[35] *Bruscamente ... anteriores* Suddenly, with a passionate vehemence that destroys the serenity of her previous words

RICARDO

¡Oh Cándida! Por favor ... (*Ella está sentada en el sofá.* RICARDO *pasea por el fondo ante la terraza. Cándida sofoca unos suaves sollozos. Se seca unas pocas lágrimas. Y en seguida busca con los ojos a su marido y le sonríe.*)

CÁNDIDA

¡Ea! ya está. No te asustes. No voy a hacerte una escena ...
5 (RICARDO *avanza y se sienta junto a ella en el sofá.*)

RICARDO

¡Cándida! Yo soy un sinvergüenza.

CÁNDIDA (*Un suspiro*)

Si esperas que yo te lleve la contraria ...[36]

RICARDO

¡Pero no puedo cambiar!

CÁNDIDA

¡Hombre! Por lo menos, no me lo digas ...

RICARDO

10 No. No puedo cambiar ... Es inútil. Lo he intentado muchísimas veces. Pero este modo de ser mío es algo superior a mi propia voluntad.[37] ¿Y sabes por qué, Cándida? Porque me asusta dejar de ser joven ...

CÁNDIDA

¡Oh!

---

[36] *Si esperas ... contraria* Don't expect me to contradict you
[37] *Pero ... voluntad* But my nature is stronger than my will

RICARDO

Cuando pienso que tengo muchas canas, que nuestros hijos han crecido, que el tiempo pasa y no vuelve, cuando pienso todo eso, Cándida, me echo a temblar y me lanzo a una nueva aventura, tan estúpida como todas, sólo para convencerme a mí mismo de que todavía soy joven ... Yo no tengo la culpa, Cándida. ¡La vida es tan hermosa para los que aún son jóvenes! ¡Es tan difícil renunciar! Ten paciencia, Cándida. Todo esto pasará ... ¿Me comprendes un poco? ¿Puedes comprenderme? 5

CÁNDIDA

¿Por qué no?

RICARDO

¡Eres una santa! 10

CÁNDIDA

No me llames santa ... Es un piropo muy triste. (*Sonríe.*) Anda. Más tarde seguiremos hablando. Ahora, lo mejor será que te acuestes un rato. Lo necesitas.

RICARDO

¡Sí! Estoy destrozado. Figúrate ... No he pegado un ojo.

CÁNDIDA

No me cuentes detalles. 15

RICARDO

¡Je! Perdona ... (RICARDO *le besa una mano y marcha hacia la puerta. Allí se vuelve.*) Buenos noches.

CÁNDIDA (*Corrigiendo con suavidad*)

Buenos días.

RICARDO

¡Ah! ¡Claro! Es verdad ... Buenos días.

(*Sale* RICARDO *definitivamente. Queda* CÁNDIDA *sola, mirando a la puerta por donde salió. Muy aprisa, casi corriendo, entra* MANOLITA *por el fondo. Viene de la calle, quitándose los guantes apresuradamente. Viste bien.* 5 *Es bonita.*)

MANOLITA

¡Buenos días, señora! ¿Cómo está usted? ¡Ay, no me diga nada![38] Ya sé que vengo tarde. Pero no es mía la culpa. ¡Si usted supiera! Don Ricardo debe de estar furioso, como si lo viera,[39] y con razón. Con el geniecito que se le pone al ilustre abogado[40] cuando tiene que 10 dictar algo urgente y no ha llegado la mecanógrafa. Y conste que yo soy una mecanógrafa de las más cumplidoras; pero hoy ...

CÁNDIDA (*Mirándola*)

¿Que le ocurre, Manolita?

MANOLITA (*Desconcertada*)

¿Qué? No comprendo ...

CÁNDIDA

Parece que no tiene usted buen aspecto ...

MANOLITA

15 ¡Ay! Pero ¿cómo me lo ha notado usted? Si me he maquillado muchísimo ...

CÁNDIDA

Por eso. Usted no se maquilla nunca. ¿Es que ha dormido poco?

---

[38] ¡*Ay, no me diga nada*! Oh, please don't scold me!
[39] *como si lo viera* I can just see him
[40] *Con ... abogado* The famous lawyer has a fit

MANOLITA

¡Qué lista es usted! No he dormido nada ...

CÁNDIDA

¿Nada?

MANOLITA

¡Nada!

CÁNDIDA

¡Ah, vamos! Ya sabía yo ... Una mala noche ...

MANOLITA

¡Oh, no! No puedo decir eso. Ha sido una noche maravillosa. 5

CÁNDIDA

¿Acompañada?

MANOLITA

¡Claro! Eso no se pregunta. Las mujeres a solas no somos nunca felices.[41] Los hombres, sí, porque son más egoístas.

CÁNDIDA

Ya ... (*Despacio*) ¿Era ... casado?

MANOLITA (*Impresionada*)

¿Cómo lo ha adivinado usted? 10

CÁNDIDA

Porque los solteros ahora no salen de noche. Son muy serios.

---

[41] *Las mujeres ... felices* We women are never happy all by ourselves

MANOLITA

Sí; era casado.

CÁNDIDA

Entonces, ya me lo figuro todo .... Primero la llevó a cenar a un restaurante de lujo que está instalado imitando una taberna baratita ...

MANOLITA (*Sorprendida*)

5 ¡Sí!

CÁNDIDA

Hacia las doce fueron ustedes a bailar a una *boîte* ... ¿No es eso?

MANOLITA

Sí, sí ... Eso mismo.

CÁNDIDA

Luego, en el coche la llevó a un sitio de las afueras, que no cierra en toda la noche. Bebieron champán, naturalmente. El le contó su vida.
10 Cuando bebe un poco tiene muchísimo ángel. Es muy gracioso. Usted se reía como una chiquilla. ¿No es verdad? Después, cuando se hizo de día, fueron a desayunar a una de esas chocolaterías de bajos fondos, muy típicas. Total, que apenas hace un ratito[42] él la dejó en la puerta de su casa. Usted sólo ha tenido el tiempo justo de
15 arreglarse un poco, y aquí está. Porque, eso, sí, usted es una chica muy cumplidora. ¡Ah! Me olvidaba de lo más importante. Cuando iban ustedes por la carretera, de madrugada, el paró el coche y la besó ...

MANOLITA

Pero, señora ... (*Asustada*) ¿Cómo lo sabe usted todo?

---

[42] *apenas hace un ratito* scarcely a moment ago

CÁNDIDA

Porque me lo contó otra mecanógrafa que tuvo mi marido antes que usted ... ¿O es que creía usted que era la primera? ¡Estúpida!

MANOLITA

Señora, por Dios ... ¡Qué vergüenza! Me muero de vergüenza. No todo es como usted cree ... Yo le diré ...

(*Entra, muy aprisa,* TONY, *contentísimo, vestido con su impecable traje de jugador de tenis. Se planta alegremente, presumido, ante su madre.*) 5

TONY

Oye, mamá. Mírame bien. ¿No crees que estoy como para una fotografía?[43] ¿Eh? (*Silencio.* TONY, *al advertir la actitud de su madre, se vuelve y descubre a* MANOLITA.) ¡Ah! Perdón ... Buenos días, Manolita.

MANOLITA

Buenos días. (*De pronto,* MANOLITA *prorrumpe en un sollozo ahogado y escapa corriendo por el fondo. El muchacho se vuelve estupefacto hacia su madre.*) 10

TONY

¡Mamá! ... ¿Qué ha pasado? (CÁNDIDA, *con los nervios rotos, ya en plena crisis, se deja caer en el sofá y rompe en sollozos incontenibles. Oculta el rostro entre las manos.* TONY *acude.*) ¡Mamá! Pero, ¡mamá ...! ¿Qué te ocurre? ¡Dime por qué lloras! 15

CÁNDIDA (*Ruborizada*)

Calla, Tony, calla.

TONY

Dilo, mamá.

---

[43] *¿No crees ... fotografía?* Don't you think I look good enough to be photographed?

CÁNDIDA

Tony, hijo ...

(*Un nuevo sollozo. Se refugia en los brazos de* TONY. *El muchacho la acaricia con ternura. Entra* MAITÉ. *Viene con un libro, recitando a media voz su lección.*)

MAITÉ

5 "J'ai aimé. Tu as aimé. Il a aimé ... Nous avons aimé. Vous avez aimé ..."[44]

TONY

¿Te quieres callar?

MAITÉ

¿Qué sucede?

TONY

¿No lo ves? ¡Que mamá está llorando! (*En pie, mirando, airadamente*
10 *la puerta por donde salió* MANOLITA.) Y estoy seguro de que la culpa la tiene papá!

CÁNDIDA

¡Silencio, Tony! No te permito que juzgues a tu padre ...

TONY

¡Mamá!

CÁNDIDA

¿No me has oído?

TONY

15 Está bien, mamá.

(*Sale* TONY *con coraje.* MAITÉ *va hacia* CÁNDIDA. *Se arrodilla a su lado, en la alfombra.*)

---

[44] "*J'ai aimé ... avez aimé*" I loved. You loved. He loved ... We loved. You loved ..." (French conjugation of the verb "aimer" in the past)

MAITÉ

Tía ..., tía Cándida. Anda, mujer, no te preocupes. Conmigo puedes llorar todo lo que quieras. ¿Crees que no lo sé todo? Tú te pasas la vida disimulando lo que te hacen sufrir las andanzas del tío Ricardo, para que los chicos y yo y las criadas y las visitas no sepamos lo que sufres y lo que lloras. ¿Y sabes por qué, tía Cándida? Porque eres muy orgullosa, mucho, muchísimo, y te daría mucha rabia que tuviéramos compasión de ti. No lo niegues ... Si lo que a una se le escape.[45] Pero bien lloras cuando te quedas solita en tu cuarto, cada vez que tío Ricardo no viene por la noche, o se va de viaje diciendo que tiene que defender un pleito en Barcelona; como si no supiera una que se va al Escorial, y en El Escorial, en vez de pleitos, lo que hay son líos ...[46] Anda, tía, ahora que estamos solas, ¿por qué no me haces confidencias de mujer a mujer?[47]

CÁNDIDA

Pero, chiquilla ... (*La mira y sonríe.*) ¡Por Dios!

MAITÉ

¿Por qué no me lo dices todo a mí solita? ¿Verdad que estás enamoradísima de tu marido y tienes unos celos horribles?

CÁNDIDA (*Acariciándola*)

Sí, pequeña. Le quiero. Le quiero con toda mi alma. No es malo, ¿sabes, Maité? Es un chiquillo. Un chiquillo travieso que hace daño y hace llorar,[48] sin querer hacer daño y sin conocer siquiera el valor de una lágrima, porque él no ha llorado nunca. A veces, me gustaría no quererle tanto, para no perdonarle; para que él también sufriera un poco. Pero es inútil ... No puedo. Le quiero. Cuando me mira, ya no tengo fuerzas para reñirle ...

---

[45] *Si lo que ... escape* These things don't escape me

[46] *en vez ... líos* instead of law intrigues he has love affairs (a play on the words *pleito* and *lío*)

[47] *¿por qué ... mujer?* why don't you confide in me as one woman to another?

[48] *que hace ... llorar* who hurts and makes one cry

MAITÉ

Si no me extraña. Si es que el muy golfo tiene un ángel ...

CÁNDIDA (*Escandalizada*)

¡Maité! ¡No hables así de tu tío!

MAITÉ

Vamos, tía. Yo sé lo que digo. Al tío Ricardo no le falla una.[49] Mis amigas están todas chifladas por él. Maruja Roldán le hace versos,
5 no te digo más.[50] Y Lolita le escribe anónimos. Sin mala intención, desde luego, porque Lolita es muy decente ...

CÁNDIDA

Ya, ya. Si he leído esos anónimos. Lo que pasa es que, como Lolita le escribe sin firmar, le dice todo lo que le diría si no fuera tan decente como es. Y no quieras saber.[51]

MAITÉ

10 Es que así se desahoga la pobre,[52] ¿sabes? Lolita es una chica de la nueva generación y tiene recursos para todo. Vosotras, en cambio, las señoras de tu edad, sois una calamidad ...

CÁNDIDA

¡Niña!

MAITÉ

¡Sí, sí! No protestes. Y tú más que ninguna. Una calamidad, buení-
15 sima y guapísima. Un encanto de calamidad. Pero lo eres. ¿Qué has hecho tú para impedir que tu marido se te escape hoy con una y mañana con otra?

---

[49] *Al tío ... falla una* They all fall for Uncle Richard
[50] *no te digo más* (*coll.*) I'll have you know
[51] *Y no quieras saber* (*coll.*) Just imagine (what she says)
[52] *Es que ... pobre* Why, that's the way the poor thing gets rid of her frustrations

CÁNDIDA

¡Yo le he querido con toda mi alma!

MAITÉ

¡Ay, qué graciosa!

CÁNDIDA

¡Niña!

MAITÉ

Está visto que las señoras casadas no entendéis una palabra del matrimonio ... 5

CÁNDIDA (*Mirándola con espanto*)

¿Tú crees?

MAITÉ (*Muy maternal*)

¡Qué inocente eres, tía! Una mujer siempre tiene en su mano muchísimos recursos para evitar que un hombre se le escape. Aunque sea el marido, que es el que más motivos tiene para escaparse ... Te lo digo yo, que de esto entiendo un rato.[53] 10

CÁNDIDA

¿Tú?

MAITÉ

¡Huy! La mar ... ¿Has probado a darle celos a tu marido alguna vez?

CÁNDIDA

¿Yo? (*Con indignación*) ¿Por quién me tomas?

[53] *Te lo digo ... rato* Take it from me who knows a lot about such things

MAITÉ

¿Es que has flirteado con sus amigos?

CÁNDIDA (*Horrorizada*)

¡¡Nunca!! ¡Me hubiera muerto de vergüenza!

MAITÉ

Es que, por lo menos, has tenido uno de esos amigos íntimos que tienen muchas señoras para contarle a él las cosas íntimas que
5 no se le pueden contar al marido?

CÁNDIDA

¡No! ¡Jamás! Todos mis pensamientos han sido para él ... Hasta mis sueños.

MAITÉ (*Con bondadosa reconvención*)

Pero, tía ... ¿No sabes que el primer deber de una mujer casada es tener en vilo al marido?[54]

CÁNDIDA (*Mirándola, horrorizada*)

10 ¡Ay, ay, Dios mío! ¿Quién te ha enseñado todo eso?

MAITÉ

Claro que todavía estás a tiempo. Porque, no sé si lo sabrás, pero estás guapísima. De manera que, si te decides, el pobre tío Ricardo va a andar de coronilla ...[55]

CÁNDIDA (*En pie. Un grito*)

¡Basta, Maité!

MAITÉ (*Asustadísima*)

15 ¡Tía Cándida!

---

[54] *tener en vilo al marido* to keep the husband dangling (in suspense)
[55] *el pobre ... coronilla* poor Uncle Richard is going to be kept hopping

CÁNDIDA

¡He dicho que te calles! ¡Ni una palabra más! No sé cómo he podido escucharte sin darte una bofetada. Pero ¿quién ha educado a esta mocosa? Por supuesto, ¿quién va a ser?[56] ¡Su tío!

MAITÉ

¡Tía Cándida!

CÁNDIDA

¡Que te calles! ¡Y ésta es la nueva generación! 5

MAITÉ

Pero, tía ...

CÁNDIDA

¡Silencio! ¡Proponerme que flirtee con los amigos de mi marido! ¡A mí! ¡Qué horror! Querer convertirme en una de esas casadas de ahora que viven con sus maridos la misma vida que antes vivían los maridos con sus amantes. De fiesta en fiesta, de cabaret en cabaret. 10 Con un vestido por aquí y por allí ... Y a beber. Y a bailar. A bailar con los amigos del marido, claro, porque con el marido no tiene interés; ya se comprende. (*Se vuelve furiosa hacia la muchacha.*) ¿Es eso lo que quieres de mí? ¡Dilo!

MAITÉ

¡Claro! Pero no sé por qué te pones así. Si todo eso es de primer 15 año ...[57]

CÁNDIDA

¡Descarada!

MAITÉ

¡Ay, tía!

---

[56] *¿quién va a ser?* who else could it be?

[57] *Pero no sé ... primer año* But I don't know why you have to get so angry. It's all so elementary

CÁNDIDA

¡Vete! Déjame. Quiero estar sola ...

MAITÉ

Bueno. Me iré. (*Refunfuñando*) La culpa la tiene una por meterse a arreglar matrimonios ...

(*Muy mohina, entra en la terraza. Desde allí, durante los momentos que* 5 *siguen, observa atentamente, tras los cristales, la actitud de* CÁNDIDA, *que ha quedado en el sofá, vuelta de espaldas a la terraza, y habla en su interrumpido monólogo. Pero a poco va transformándose su tono de irritación por otro de desaliento y de amargura.*)[58]

CÁNDIDA

Sí; ya sé, ya sé. Conozco muy bien a esa clase de mujeres. Esas, esas 10 son las que tienen el marido a sus pies: con sus mimos, con sus carantoñas, con sus frivolidades. Tienen amigos, coquetean con ellos. Juegan con el peligro sin quemarse. Una mirada es como un beso. ¡Ah! Pero un beso es inmoral, casi un adulterio. Una mirada no es nada ... Ni siquiera pecado. ¿Quién puede decir nada de una 15 señora tan encantadora? Así triunfan, un día y otro. ¡Siempre! Y, mientras, el pobre marido, con los ojos bien abiertos, vigilándola, mimándola, como un esclavo, para que no se le escape, para no perderla ... (*Un hondísimo suspiro*) ¡Quién fuera como ellas![59] (*Un silencio. Parece que responde a una sugerencia ajena.*) ¡Qué tontería! Pero 20 si sería inútil. Si no sé. Soy una ignorante. Una pobre mujer tonta y anticuada. ¡Pobre de mí! Yo coqueteando ... Por Dios. Sería ridículo, ridículo. (*Otro silencio.* MAITÉ, *desde la terraza, la observa. El rostro de* CÁNDIDA, *respondiendo a sus pensamientos, se transfigura lentamente. Y, sin moverse, llama. Primero, bajito. Luego, más fuerte.*) ¡Maité! 25 ¡Maité! (MAITÉ *corre desde la terraza y llega a su lado.*)

MAITÉ

¡Aquí estoy!

---

[58] *Pero ... de amargura* But gradually her irritation is transformed into discouragement and bitterness

[59] *¡Quién fuera como ellas!* Oh, to be like them!

CÁNDIDA

Ven aquí, hija. Acércate ... ¿De verdad crees que todo lo que has dicho antes es cierto? ¿Estás segura de que tu tío volvería a mí si tuviera celos, si tuviera miedo de perderme?

MAITÉ

¡Segurísima! ¡Eso no ha fallado nunca!

CÁNDIDA (*Muy avergonzada*)

Entonces, si tú, que tienes tantísima experiencia, me das algunas lecciones podíamos hacer la prueba ... 5

MAITÉ (*Entusiasmada*)

¡Bravo!

CÁNDIDA

En este momento soy capaz de cualquier locura.

MAITÉ

¡Bravísimo, tiita! ¡Así me gusta! Lo que nos vamos a divertir[60] cuando el tío Ricardo se entere ... (*Transición*) Ahora, lo más urgente es buscar un hombre digno de ti ... 10

CÁNDIDA

Pero ¿me lo vas a buscar tú?

MAITÉ

¡Naturalmente! Tú no tienes ninguna práctica y harías una tontería ...[61]

CÁNDIDA

Es verdad ... No tengo costumbre. 15

---

[60] *Lo que ... divertir* What a good time we're going to have

[61] *Tú no tienes ... tontería* You've had no experience in such matters and you'd do something foolish

MAITÉ

Tratándose de ti, que eres una verdadera señora, hay que procurar que te haga la corte un hombre que esté bien. Si es un cualquiera, cuando se entere tu marido le va a sentar muy mal ...[62]

CÁNDIDA

Bueno. Pero, por favor, que ese hombre sea un caballero ...[63] Vamos,
5 que no se aproveche.

MAITÉ

No seas ingenua. Todos los hombres se aprovechan ...

CÁNDIDA (*Con terror*)

¿Todos?

MAITÉ

¡Todos! Te lo digo yo.

CÁNDIDA

¡Ah! Entonces no quiero. ¡De ningún modo!

MAITÉ (*Severa*)

10 ¡Tía Cándida! ¿Quieres reconquistar a tu marido, sí o no?

CÁNDIDA

¡Ay, hija mía! Es que me estoy poniendo nerviosísima ...

MAITÉ

¡Con esos miramientos no vamos a ninguna parte,[64] tía Cándida! No se trata de nada inmoral. Se trata de jugar un poco a un juego que juegan muchas señoras ... Irás a todas partes del brazo de un
15 hombre distinguido, guapo ...

---

[62] *le va a sentar muy mal* he's not going to like it
[63] *que ese hombre sea un caballero* make certain that the man is a gentleman
[64] *¡Con esos miramientos ... parte ... !* We'll never get anywhere with those precautions ... !

CÁNDIDA (*Rápida*)

Bueno. No es necesario que sea guapo. Ya me arreglaré yo con lo que haya ...[65]

MAITÉ (*Indignada*)

¿Qué dices? A tío Ricardo no le puedes dar celos con una birria ...

CÁNDIDA

¿Tú crees que sería faltarle al respeto?

MAITÉ

¡Desde luego! Precisamente, lo que no perdona ningún marido es que el otro sea más feo que él. Es una cuestión de prestigio ... 5

CÁNDIDA (*Resignada*)

Está bien. Decididamente, haré todo lo que tú digas ... Pero, hija mía, ¿dónde está ese hombre con el que tengo que flirtear para dar celos a mi marido? ¿Sabes ya dónde encontrarlo? ¿Quién es? (*En este instante surge* ROSITA *en el fondo.*) 10

ROSITA

Con permiso. Señorita Maité, su profesor de francés acaba de llegar ...

(*Sale* ROSITA. MAITÉ, *al oírla, se ha puesto en pie, acometida de una inspiración repentina. Los ojos le brillan. Mira a su tía fijamente.*)

MAITÉ

¡Tía Cándida! 15

CÁNDIDA (*Adivinando. Aterrada*)

¡Hija! ¿Qué estás pensando? (MAITÉ, *sin hablar, echa a correr y desaparece por el fondo.*) ¿Eh? ¿A dónde vas? ¿Qué vas a hacer? ¡Maité! Por Dios ... ¡Ay, ay, ay!

(*Está unos segundos sola, nerviosísima. No está quieta. Va de un lado a otro. Al fin, bajo del dintel del fondo aparece la figura de* MARCELO DUVAL. 20 *Es un hombre extraño y atractivo a un tiempo. Muy tímido. Viste con un terrible desaliño. Habla con muy marcado acento francés. Bastante azarado, queda un poco en la puerta sin hablar.*)

---

[65] *Ya me ... lo que haya* I'll settle for whatever there is

MARCELO

Buenos días, "madame." Maité dice que me necesita usted urgentemente ...

CÁNDIDA

¿Eh? ¡Usted! ¡Usted! "monsieur" Duval! (*Le mira de arriba abajo y de pronto rompe en una risa franca, clara, alegre, incontenible.* MARCELO, *naturalmente, se la queda mirando atónito. Una pausa. Ella sigue riendo.* MARCELO, *muy azorado, se mira a sí mismo buscando el motivo de tan evidente regocijo.*)

MARCELO

"Madame!"

CÁNDIDA (*Sin dejar de reir*)

¡Ay! ¡Usted! ¡Usted! Nunca se me hubiera ocurrido. (*Y sigue riendo con toda su alma*[66] *ante la estupefacción de* MARCELO. *Éste vuelve a mirarse. Al fin, aunque muy impresionado, da un paso con mucha timidez.*)

MARCELO

¡Señora! ¿De verdad resulto tan gracioso?

(*Entran en tropel, por el fondo,* MAITÉ, MANOLÍN *y* TONY. *Con mucha algazara rodean a* CÁNDIDA, *a un lado de la escena. Al otro, muy distante, siempre en la luna,* MARCELO.)

TONY

¡Colosal, mamá! Ya nos lo ha explicado Maité. Me parece muy bien que le des a papá una lección.[67] Después de todo, si te autorizamos nosotros, la cosa no puede ser más decente ...

MAITÉ (*Mostrándole con el ademán, orgullosamente, a* MARCELO)

¿Eh? ¿Qué te parece?

---

[66] *Y sigue ... su alma* And she continues laughing heartily
[67] *Me parece ... lección* I think it's fine that you should teach dad a lesson

MANOLÍN (*Muy decidido*)

¿Vale éste o buscamos otro?[68]

TONY (*Con ojo de experto*)

No tiene mala facha. Es agradable ...

MARCELO (*Asombradísimo*)

¿Se refieren ustedes a mí?

MAITÉ

¡Claro! ¿A quién va a ser?[69]

MARCELO (*Boquiabierto*)

Es asombroso, asombroso. 5

MAITÉ

Me parece que éste es el hombre que te conviene ... ¿Te gusta?

TONY

Di, mamá, ¿te gusta?

MANOLÍN

¿Te gusta?

MARCELO

Dígalo, señora, que no puedo más. ¿Le gusto?

CÁNDIDA (*Sin atreverse a mirarle. Muy bajito*)

Pues ... , sí. 10

LOS TRES MUCHACHOS (*Aplaudiendo*)

¡Bravo! ¡Bravo!

MAITÉ

¡Le gusta!

---

[68] *¿Vale éste ... otro?* Will this one do, or shall we look for another?
[69] *¿A quién va a ser?* Who else?

MANOLÍN

¡Le gusta!

TONY

¡Le gusta!

MARCELO

¿De veras le gusto? Es emocionante. (MAITÉ *se abraza a su tía.* TONY *y* MANOLÍN *pasan al lado de Marcelo y le estrechan la mano efusivamente, con*
5 *gran entusiasmo.*)

TONY

¡Enhorabuena, "monsieur" Duval! Le gusta usted.

MARCELO

Gracias.

MANOLÍN

Le felicito, profesor. ¡Chóquela! Y conste que mamá no habla por cumplir. Cuando ella dice que usted le gusta, es que le gusta.

MARCELO (*Atónito*)

10 Gracias, muchas gracias. Me siento muy orgulloso de gustarle a su señora mamá. Estoy encantado. Pero, en fin, nunca hubiera podido sospecharlo. "Oh, mon Dieu!" ¡Qué día!

CÁNDIDA

Más tarde le explicaremos a usted el juego, "monsieur" Duval ... Porque supongo que, en principio, todo esto le parecerá a usted una
15 inmoralidad.[70]

MARCELO

¿Una inmoralidad? A mí no, "madame." ¡Yo soy francés!

LOS TRES MUCHACHOS (*Entusiasmados*)

¡Bravo!

TELÓN

[70] *todo esto ... inmoralidad* all this must seem very immoral to you

Acto Segundo

El mismo decorado. Quince días después. Una noche, de madrugada.

MANOLÍN, tumbado en el sofá, duerme profundamente. En el suelo, junto al sofá, hay varios libros caídos, lo que denota que el sueño le acometió en medio del estudio. Entra ROSITA llevando una bandejita con un vaso de leche. Se detiene ante el durmiente y llama para despertarlo. 5

ROSITA

¡Señorito, Manolín!

MANOLÍN (*Incorporándose súbito*)

¿Eh? ¡Rosita!

ROSITA

Conque los libros en el suelo y durmiendo, ¿eh? ¡Así estudia usted! 10

MANOLÍN

Calla, mujer. Si es que me aburro ... Tú verás. Papá no ha cenado en casa; mamá ha salido con el profesor de francés; Maité está en casa de Lolita, y Tony se fue con un amigo. Y yo, aquí en este sofá, pasando la velada solo como único representante del hogar cristiano. Así no hay quien pueda con el Siglo de Oro.[1] 15

[1] *Así ... de Oro* No one can be expected to cope with the Golden Age under these conditions

ROSITA

¡Valiente perezoso! Si al menos no tuviera tantas picardías ...[2] (*Le muestra con enojo un papelito doblado.*) ¿Puedo saber cuándo va usted a cansarse de poner anónimos amorosos en mi mesilla de noche?

MANOLÍN

¡Qué mal pensada eres![3] Si son anónimos, ¿cómo sabes que son
5 míos?

ROSITA

Porque le he pillado el truco. Estas cartas las copia usted de un libro que se titula "Cien cartas de amor." Lo malo es que esta vez, sin darse cuenta, ha copiado usted hasta los nombres. Y este anónimo empieza: "A Josefina." Y termina: "Napoleón."

MANOLÍN (*Muy avergonzado*)

10 ¡Caray! ¡Qué despiste!

ROSITA

Y vamos. Desde luego, yo no soy esa doña Josefina. Pero lo que es usted Napoleón, ya, ya ...[4]

MANOLÍN

Si es que me tienes loco, Rosita.

ROSITA (*Enfadada*)

¿Quiere usted no decir más desvergüenzas? Tómese su vaso de leche,
15 y a la cama.

MANOLÍN (*Amargamente*)

¡Cómo me humillas, Rosita! ¡El vaso de leche todas las noches y el hipofosfitos todas las mañanas! ¡Maldita sea!

---

[2] *Si al menos ... picardías* If you at least didn't misbehave so much
[3] ¡ *Qué mal pensada eres*! What a suspicious mind you have!
[4] *Pero ... Napoleón, ya, ya* But as for your being Napoleon! Now, really!

ROSITA

¡Señorito! ¡Señorito!

(*Entra* TONY, *muy contento. Al poco, sale* ROSITA.)

TONY

Oye, Manolín. ¿Te acuerdas de Piluca Montes?

MANOLÍN

Aquella morena que conocimos este verano en Zarauz?

TONY

La misma. Me ha acompañado hasta aquí, y, abajo, en el portal, al despedirnos, me ha pedido relaciones ... [5] 5

MANOLÍN

¡Atiza!

TONY

Como lo oyes.

MANOLÍN

Le has dado esperanzas?

TONY

Hombre, yo, para que no viera que lo estaba deseando, le he dicho que lo pensaré. Pero mañana le diré que sí. Estamos citados en el Retiro. Pero no se lo digas a Maité. Ya sabes que no me deja tener novia ... (*Muy contento*) Bueno. ¿Qué te parece? 10

MANOLÍN (*Sensato*)

Si la chica va con buen fin ... [6]

TONY

Yo creo que sí. Parece muy formal. 15

---

[5] *me ha pedido relaciones* she has asked me to go steady

[6] *Si la chica ... buen fin* If the girl's intentions are honorable

MANOLÍN

Entonces, enhorabuena, chico. ¡Qué suerte tienes!

TONY (*Modestamente*)

Hombre ... ¡Psch!

MANOLÍN

Pero ¿qué quieres que te diga?[7] A mí me hubiera gustado más vivir en otros tiempos ... Cuando se declaraban los hombres a las mujeres
5 ... ¡Qué bien lo hubiera hecho yo! (*En este momento entra* ROSITA. MANOLÍN, *embargado por el más impetuoso ardor caballeresco, se lanza a sus pies, rodilla en tierra, toma una mano de la muchacha y declama.*) ¡Rosita! ¡Princesa mía! Te amo.

ROSITA

¡Y dale!

MANOLÍN

10 Ojos de cielo, cara de rosa, boca de fresa ... ¿Puedo besar tu bella mano?

ROSITA

¡Psch! (*Con resignación*) Si no es más que la mano ...

MANOLÍN (*Besándole la mano muy apasionado*)

¡Hum! ¿Puedo besar tus lindos labios?

ROSITA

¡Ca! Eso ni lo sueñe.

MANOLÍN (*Indignado*)

15 ¡A la porra! Se estropeó la escena.

[7] *¿ qué quieres que te diga?* do you want my opinion?

ROSITA

Y no me venga con más pillerías, señorito Manolín. ¡Le he dicho que no y no![8]

(*Sale* ROSITA. MANOLÍN *se queda francamente chasqueado.*)

MANOLÍN

Está visto que esta chica no se pone en situación ... [9]

TONY (*Riendo*)

Paciencia, hombre. 5

(*Entra* MAITÉ. *Como Tony, también viene de la calle.*)

MAITÉ

¡Hola, chicos! He estado en el Capitol, con Lolita y su tía Isabel. Hemos visto una película de "gangsters." Pero, hijo, qué "gangsters." Brutotes, brutotes. ¡Estupendos! Una película colosal. Pero al final, ¡pum! la desilusión ... 10

TONY

¡Qué pasa al final?

MAITÉ

¡Que a los "gangsters" los coge la Policía!

TONY

¡Oh!

MAITÉ

Claro que esas cosas no pasan más que en América ... (*Transición*) ¿Ha vuelto vuestra madre? 15

[8] ¡ *Le he dicho que no y no*! I said "no" and I mean "no"!

[9] *esta chica ... situación* this girl is going to be difficult (*i.e.*, she is not going to be an easy conquest)

MANOLÍN

¡Ca! Telefoneó diciendo que no la esperáramos. Fue con el profesor de francés a dar un paseo por el Madrid antiguo ...

MAITÉ

¡Otra vez!

MANOLÍN

Otra vez. Por lo visto es un capricho ...

MAITÉ (*Indignada*)

5 ¡Pero eso es absurdo!

TONY

Mujer ... Tanto como absurdo.[10] Dicen que el Madrid antiguo es muy bonito. Yo he visto fotografías ...

MAITÉ

Pero es que siguiendo por ese camino,[11] tía Cándida y "monsieur" Duval se irán un día a Toledo ...

TONY

10 Pues mira. Parece que Toledo tampoco está mal. Los sudamericanos cuentan y no acaban ...[12]

MAITÉ

¡No lo digo por eso! Lo que me parece una torpeza es que tía Cándida y el profesor se pasen las noches en el Madrid antiguo, las tardes en el Retiro y las mañanas en el Museo del Prado ... Tres
15 sitios a donde no va nadie. (*Muy enfadada*) ¿Será posible que vuestra madre no sepa sostener un "flirt" ni siquiera por las apariencias?

[10] *Tanto como absurdo* I wouldn't call it absurd
[11] *Pero es que ... camino* But if they continue that way
[12] *Los sudamericanos ... no acaban* Latin Americans never stop talking about it

MANOLÍN

¡La pobrecilla no tiene práctica!

TONY

¡Es que es más inocente!

MAITÉ

Vuestra madre tiene que hacer precisamente todo lo contrario de lo que está haciendo. Nada de paseítos románticos a la luz de la luna ... Tonterías. Nada de visitas al Museo del Prado. Eso se queda para las inglesas. Ella es española, a Dios gracias. Tienen que verla del brazo de monsieur Duval para que la gente critique y se lo cuenten al tío Ricardo. Pero que la vean en los sitios donde va la gente elegante: en los estrenos, en las "boîtes," en las tabernas ... Lo natural. ¿No hemos empezado esta comedia para que tío Ricardo tenga celos y vuelva a enamorarse de ella? Os aseguro que yo no estaré tranquila hasta que vea cómo tío Ricardo le suelta una bofetada a monsieur Duval. ...

TONY (*Muy contento*)

¡Será emocionante!

MANOLÍN (*También*)

¡Con los puños que tiene papá![13]

MAITÉ

Pues ya veis ... Llevamos así quince días y vuestro padre sin enterarse.[14] ¿Dónde ha comido tío Ricardo esta noche?

TONY

En el Círculo, con un señor de Bilbao ...

---

[13] *¡Con los puños que tiene papá!* Considering dad's huge fists!

[14] *Llevamos ... sin enterarse* We've been at this for two weeks and your dad isn't even aware of it

MAITÉ

¡Ay, qué fresco! De juerga.

TONY

¿Tú crees?

MAITÉ

Seguro. Los señores de Bilbao no fallan nunca ...[15]

(*Entra* ROSITA. *Trae, en una bandeja, un frasco de "whisky," una botella de soda y dos vasos. Calladamente, lo dispone todo en una mesita junto al sofá. Los muchachos la rodean con evidente curiosidad.*)

TONY

¡Rosita!

MANOLÍN

"¿Whisky?"

ROSITA

"Whisky." Es orden de la señora. Acaba de llegar con el profesor y me mandó que preparara aquí algo para beber ...

MAITÉ

¿Dónde están?

ROSITA

En el despacho, buscando una "Guía Turística de España" ...

MAITÉ

¡Ay! Cuando yo digo que se van a Toledo ... (*Sale* ROSITA. *De pronto,* MAITÉ *chilla.* MANOLÍN *y* TONY *pegan un respingo de susto.*) ¡¡Ay!!

MANOLÍN

¡Contra!

[15] *Los señores ... nunca* The gentlemen from Bilbao never fail him as a good excuse (*i.e.*, as a "business" appointment)

TONY

Oye, tú ...

MAITÉ (*Iluminada*)

¡No digáis nada! ¡No habléis! ¡Dejadme pensar! ¡¡Sí!! Esta es la ocasión. ¡Y qué ocasión! Figuraos la escena ...

MANOLÍN (*Asombradísimo*)

¿Qué escena?

MAITÉ

¡Esta! (*Mira en torno sugestionada.*) El salón a media luz. Dos vasos de "whisky." Tía Cándida y el profesor de francés sentados en ese sofá muy juntos, hablando en voz baja. Y en ese momento ... 5

MANOLÍN Y TONY (*Con ansiedad*)

¿Qué?

MAITÉ (*Entusiasmada*)

En ese momento, entra vuestro padre y, ¡zas! se lanza sobre monsieur Duval y empieza a darle puñetazos ... 10

MANOLÍN (*Enardecido*)

¡Bravo!

TONY

!Imponente!

MAITÉ (*Complacidísima*)

¿Verdad que es una buena ocurrencia?

TONY (*Transición*)

Oye. Pero ¿cómo va a venir papá si no sabe que mamá y el otro están aquí? 15

MAITÉ

Lo sabrá y vendrá. De eso me encargo yo ...[16] ¿No dices que tu padre está en el Círculo?

TONY

¡Sí!

MAITÉ

Venid. Vamos al otro teléfono.

TONY

5 Pero ...

MAITÉ

Vamos al teléfono.

(Salen los tres. Por unos segundos, queda la escena sola. Un reloj da dos lentas campanadas. Entra CÁNDIDA *sola. Tiene cierto aire ausente y preocupado.*[17] *Muy despacio se sienta en el sofá. Prepara en los dos vasos whisky y* 10 *soda. Bebe unos sorbos y piensa ensimismada. Con un mohín nervioso clava los ojos en la puerta por donde entró. La impaciencia la hace repiquetear con un pie*[18] *sobre la alfombra. Al fin, en esa misma puerta, aparece* MARCELO. *Viene muy calmoso, leyendo con muchísima atención un pequeño librito. Es la "Guía Turística de España." Atraviesa la escena, sin dejar de leer, se sienta* 15 *también en el sofá, pero muy distante de* CÁNDIDA. *Y sigue leyendo con un interés extraordinario. Ella le observa de reojo. Así, unos instantes. De pronto,* MARCELO *alza los ojos del libro y dice muy satisfecho, con cierto aire de triunfo.)*

MARCELO

¡Toledo!

CÁNDIDA

20 ¿Cómo?

MARCELO

Mañana iremos a Toledo. Hay coche de línea por la mañana y por la tarde ... ¿Conoce usted Toledo?

---

[16] *De eso me encargo yo* I'll see to that
[17] *Tiene ... y preocupado* She appears somewhat absent-minded and worried
[18] *La impaciencia ... pie* Impatience makes her click her heel nervously

CÁNDIDA

Muy poco. (*Humildemente*) Estuve un día hace muchísimos años ...

MARCELO

¡Oh! Es maravilloso. La Catedral, la Casa del Greco,[19] la Posada, esas callecitas estrechas y empinadas ... (*Muy preocupado*) Claro que hay un inconveniente. Si mañana vamos a Toledo, no podremos hacer nuestra visita diaria al Museo del Prado. 5

CÁNDIDA (*Muy rápida*)

¡No importa!

MARCELO (*Muy amable*)

¿De verdad no le importa sacrificarse y no ir al Museo?

CÁNDIDA

¡¡No!! (*Casi feliz*) ¡Se lo juro!

MARCELO

Bien. A Toledo. (*Dichoso, hojeando la guía*) Otro día iremos a Aranjuez. Oh, "c'est un petit Versailles!"[20] Los jardines, el Palacio, el río. 10 Después, a Ávila ...

CÁNDIDA (*Impulsivamente*)

¡No!

MARCELO (*Muy contento*)

¡Sí, sí! Y también quiero enseñarle a usted Sigüenza, El Escorial ...

CÁNDIDA (*Con terror*)

¡Dios mío! Pero si conoce usted toda España ...

MARCELO

¡Señora! (*Modestamente*) Es que soy extranjero. 15

[19] *la Casa del Greco:* El Greco's house, an attraction in Toledo since it contains many of El Greco's paintings. See vocabulary under Greco

[20] "c'est un petit Versailles!" (French) it's like a Versailles in miniature!

CÁNDIDA

Pues óigame, "monsieur" Duval (*Con furiosísimo orgullo*) A los españoles, cuando somos niños, nos llevan un día a Toledo, otro a Aranjuez y otro al Escorial, y después ya no volvemos, en toda nuestra vida, ni a Toledo, ni a Aranjuez, ni al Escorial ...

MARCELO (*Asombradísimo*)

5 ¡Qué horror! Entonces, ¿cómo admiran ustedes sus monumentos nacionales?

CÁNDIDA

¡Por las postales!

MARCELO

¡Oh!

CÁNDIDA

Y si no, ¿para qué cree usted que se han inventado las postales?

MARCELO (*Anonadado*)

10 Es curioso. Muy curioso ... (*Bastante avergonzado,* MARCELO *se sienta en un extremo del sofá.* CÁNDIDA *está al otro lado de la escena, presa de verdadera indignación.*)[21]

CÁNDIDA

¡No puedo más! Es demasiado ... Son quince días yendo[22] todas las mañanas al Museo del Prado para oirle a usted decir que la pintura 15 de vanguardia empieza en los primitivos. Quince días escuchando toda clase de pruebas para convencerme que la "Maja desnuda" no es la duquesa de Alba.[23] Claro que en eso pierde usted el tiempo. Porque yo pienso lo peor, y estoy segurísima de que la "Maja desnuda" es la duquesa de Alba ...

[21] *presa de verdadera indignación* overwhelmed with genuine indignation
[22] *Son quince días yendo* We've been going for the past two weeks
[23] *la "Maja desnuda" ... de Alba* the nude "Maja" is not the Duchess of Alba (a reference to Goya's famous painting, and the supposed model, the Duchess of Alba, a highly distinguished lady of the Spanish aristocracy)

MARCELO

¡No!

CÁNDIDA

¡Sí! Es ella. Me consta. Lo sé de muy buena tinta.[24] Y Goya, un verdadero sinvergüenza. Lo que pasa es que usted le defiende porque ya se sabe que los hombres se defienden unos a otros ...

MARCELO

¡Oh, "madame"!

CÁNDIDA

Eso, por las mañanas. De noche todavía es peor. ¿Cree usted que hay mujer que resista lo que usted hace conmigo? Yo, pobre de mí, que tenía la idea de que todo lo que fuera salir del barrio de Salamanca era tanto como hacer un viaje a provincias ... [25] Yo, desde hace quince días, me paso las noches como un vagabundo, de una punta a otra de Madrid, y andando. Estoy rendida, no puedo más. Cada vez que me lleva usted a la calle del Sacramento tengo la impresión de que vamos a Burgos a pie ... (*Casi llorando*) Pues ¿y anoche, que se empeñó usted en que deberíamos estudiar a fondo el ambiente de "Fortunata y Jacinta,"[26] y para eso me hizo usted ir y volver desde Pontejos a la Puerta de Toledo,[27] pasando por la Fuentecilla? (*Con furia*) ¡Vamos!

MARCELO (*Con desconsuelo*)

Pero "madame" ... Yo creí que había resultado un paseo delicioso.

---

[24] *Lo sé de muy buena tinta* I know it on very good authority

[25] *todo lo que ... a provincias* anything outside the (fashionable) district of Salamanca was like taking a trip into the country (*i.e.*, the provinces as distinguished from the big cities like Madrid or Barcelona)

[26] "*Fortunata y Jacinta*": a novel by the famous 19th century Spanish novelist, Benito Pérez Galdós, which contains minute documentation on Madrid environment and customs

[27] *desde Pontejos ... Toledo* from Pontejos Street to Toledo crossroads (that is, from one end of the old part of Madrid to the other)

CÁNDIDA

Y, claro, ahora, como ya hemos agotado Madrid, quiere usted salir a provincias ... Pero eso sí que no.[28] ¡A provincias, no!

MARCELO (*Apuradísimo*)

"Madame!"

CÁNDIDA (*Con honda amargura*)

Y pensar que para usted, sólo para usted, durante quince días, me
5 he puesto mis mejores vestidos, mis zapatos más bonitos ... ¡Y he estrenado tres sombreros!

MARCELO (*Abrumado*)

¿Tres?

CÁNDIDA

¡Sí! Tres. Pero todo ha sido inútil. Ni una sonrisa, ni una felicitación, ni una de esas cosas tontas y graciosas que saben decir todos los
10 hombres. Nada. He ensayado todos los procedimientos para hacerle notar que estaba a su lado. Sólo deseaba un poco de atención. Pero he fracasado. A usted sólo le importan las historias viejas, las calles antiguas, los cuadros del Museo. Un cuadro de Miguel Angel[29] le recuerda a usted una anécdota de Victoria Colonna.[30] En la calle
15 del Rollo se pone usted a hablar de don Juan de Austria,[31] tan tranquilo. Y en el Retiro, en uno de esos maravillosos atardeceres del Retiro ... (*Severísima*) ¿Recuerda usted de lo que hemos hablado en el Retiro?

MARCELO (*Muy ruborizado*)

De la socialdemocracia.

---

[28] *Pero eso sí que no* But I certainly won't do that

[29] *Miguel Angel:* Michelangelo, famous Italian Renaissance painter and sculptor, especially known for his frescos in the Sistine Chapel in the Vatican

[30] *Victoria Colonna:* Vittoria Colonna, Italian poetess who supposedly had a romantic friendship with the aging Michelangelo while living in Rome

[31] *don Juan de Austria:* the dashing, illegitimate half-brother of Philip II. He fought against the Turks and won the battle of Lepanto, in which Cervantes was wounded

CÁNDIDA (*Indignada*)

¿Y no le da a usted vergüenza?

MARCELO (*Con los ojos bajos*)

Verdaderamente ...

CÁNDIDA

¡Monsieur Duval! A veces dudo de que sea usted francés.

MARCELO

Pero, "madame" ... Le juro que he nacido en Marsella ...

CÁNDIDA

Ah, vamos! Resulta que es francés, pero de provincias. ¡Claro! 5
Si no podía ser de otro modo.[32] ¡Si todos los franceses son como usted, terminaré creyendo que la galantería francesa es algo así como la leyenda negra de Francia! Porque para que usted lo sepa, señor mío ... [33] (*Orgullosamente*) En España es muy difícil que una señora salga tres días seguidos con un caballero sin que al tercer día la 10
señora tenga que pararle los pies al caballero.[34] Ya ve usted. ¡En eso sí que soy patriota!

MARCELO

"Madame!" (*Sorprendidísimo*) ¿Quiere usted decir que yo he debido hacerle a usted el amor?

CÁNDIDA (*Furiosa*)

¡No! 15

MARCELO

¡Oh!

---

[32] *Si no ... modo* Why, it couldn't be otherwise

[33] *Porque ... señor mío* Because I'll have you know, my dear sir

[34] *sin que ... caballero* without her having to put a halt to the gentleman's advances by the third day

CÁNDIDA

¿Cómo se atreve usted a pensar eso?

MARCELO

Perdóneme, "madame." Se lo suplico. (*Todo confusión*) Es horrible. No comprendo nada. Yo estoy muy confundido. Yo estoy, ¿cómo dicen ustedes? Hecho un lío. Eso es. Un lío. Primero, a esos dia-
5 bólicos muchachos se les ocurre la idea de que usted y yo finjamos un "flirt" para estimular el amor que su marido siente por usted. "C'est une idée magnifique,"[35] desde luego. Pero peligrosísima para mí, "madame." Porque su marido, por muy liberal que sea,[36] es un marido español. Y un marido español, por seguir la tradición, es
10 capaz de cualquier barbaridad. "Madame," desde hace quince días mi vida está en peligro. Y vea usted, ni siquiera podré contar después con la satisfacción de haber cumplido con mi deber. Porque ahora resulta, y bien lo veo, que "madame" no está satisfecha de mis servicios. "Madame" esperaba mucho más de un francés ... Es natural.
15 Los franceses, en el fondo, somos[37] víctimas de la propaganda. Puedo asegurarle a "madame" que en mi país hay muchísimos hombres tan poco interesantes como yo. (*Un suspiro*) ¡Pobre de mí! Me parece que nunca acabaré de entender a las mujeres ...
(*Se oye, dentro, la voz de* RICARDO *que grita estentóreamente.*)

RICARDO (*Dentro*)

20 ¡Cándida! (CÁNDIDA *y* MARCELO, *al oirlo, se ponen en pie.*)

CÁNDIDA

¡Ricardo!

MARCELO

¡Su marido!

RICARDO (*Dentro*)

¡Cándida!

---

[35] *"C'est une idée magnifique"* (French) It's a magnificent idea
[36] *por muy liberal que sea* however liberal he may be
[37] *Los franceses ... somos* We Frenchmen, in reality, are

CÁNDIDA

¿Qué sucede?

(*Va hacia la entrada del fondo. En ese momento surge* RICARDO *impetuosamente, todo descompuesto.*)

RICARDO

¡¡Cándida!! Ven aquí. Mírame a los ojos. ¡Dime la verdad! ¿Dónde está ese hombre? 5

MARCELO (*Muy fino*)

¿Se refiere usted a mí?

RICARDO

¡No diga usted tonterías! (*Le vuelve la espalda. A* CÁNDIDA) ¡Dime dónde está ese hombre que pone en peligro mi honor!

MARCELO (*Delicadamente*)

Pero si soy yo ... [38]

RICARDO

¿Se quiere usted callar? ¡¡Llámalo, Cándida!! Dile que salga, 10 porque voy a matarlo ... (*Llamando hacia el interior*) ¡Salga usted, canalla!

MARCELO

¡Pero si estoy aquí!

RICARDO

¡No!

CÁNDIDA (*Boquiabierta*)

¿A quién llamas? 15

RICARDO

¡¡Al otro!! ¡Tiene que haber otro!

[38] *Pero si soy yo* But *I* am the one (you are looking for)

CÁNDIDA

Te aseguro que en este momento no hay en casa más hombre que monsieur Duval ...

RICARDO

¿De verdad? ¿Me lo juras?

CÁNDIDA

¡Naturalmente! (RICARDO *se vuelve hacia* MARCELO, *le mira en silencio*
5 *de arriba abajo y se tranquiliza repentinamente.*)

RICARDO

Entonces, no hay duda. Se trata de una broma.

MARCELO (*Picadísimo*)

¿Cómo?

RICARDO

Porque, claro, usted no va a ser.[39] (*Muy divertido*) Me parece que me han gastado una broma. (RICARDO, *que ya respira con sosiego, se sienta*
10 *en el sofá y se seca el sudor.* CÁNDIDA *se sienta junto a él. Al otro lado, mortificadísimo, en pie,* MARCELO.) Ahora me lo explico todo.[40] Figúrate que estaba yo en el Círculo, tan tranquilo, hace unos minutos, cuando de pronto un ordenanza me trajo un recado telefónico. ¡Y qué recado! Al parecer, una voz desconocida, ¡una voz criminal!
15 ha llamado diciendo que en este momento, en mi casa, estaba en peligro mi honor ...

CÁNDIDA

¡Dios mío!

[39] *usted no va a ser* it can't be you
[40] *Ahora me lo explico todo* I see it all now

RICARDO

Yo, figúrate. Me volví loco. Ya sé, ya sé que no tengo derecho a dudar de ti ... Lo sé. Pero, sin embargo, es algo superior a uno mismo.[41] ¿Comprendes? Grito. Echo a correr. Entro aquí. (*Divertidísimo*) Y mira tú ... Resulta que el hombre que está contigo pasando la velada es monsieur Duval. (*Riendo*) ¿No tiene gracia? 5 (*Se ríe más.*) ¿Eh? ¿Qué te parece a ti? El pobre monsieur Duval, tu amante ... (RICARDO *prorrumpe en una carcajada más fuerte que las anteriores.*[42] MARCELO, *que desde hace un rato escucha humilladísimo,*[43] *con los ojos en el suelo, sufre una brusca transición y pega un puñetazo en un mueble.*)

MARCELO

¡No! (CÁNDIDA, *asustada, se pone en pie.*) 10

CÁNDIDA

¡Ay!

RICARDO

"Monsieur!"

MARCELO (*Reconcentrado*)

¡Ni una risa más![44] ¿Me oye?

RICARDO

¡Oiga!

MARCELO

¡Le digo que se calle! De manera que la posibilidad de que yo sea 15 el amante de su mujer le parece a usted algo tan cómico que sólo puede aceptarse a título de broma ... , ¿no es eso?

---

[41] *es algo ... mismo* it is something beyond my will

[42] *prorrumpe ... anteriores* he bursts out laughing more loudly than before

[43] *que desde ... humilladísimo* who, deeply humiliated, has been listening for some time

[44] ¡ *Ni una risa más*! Stop your laughter (*i.e.*, I won't stand for any more laughter from you!)

RICARDO

No he querido ofenderle.[45] (*Muy conciliador*) Por mí, tiene usted todas las condiciones necesarias para ser el amante de mi mujer ...

CÁNDIDA (*Aterrada*)

¿Qué estás diciendo?

RICARDO

Bueno. No es eso.

MARCELO (*Indignado*)

5 ¿Es que no le gusta a usted mi tipo?

RICARDO

¡Hombre! De tipo no está usted mal, y de cara, tampoco. Ya quisieran muchos.[46] (*Muy fino*) ¿A ti qué te parece, Cándida?

CÁNDIDA

A mí "monsieur" Duval me parece muy atractivo ...

RICARDO

¿Oye usted? Por parte de mi mujer tampoco hay inconveniente ...

CÁNDIDA

10 ¡Ricardo! ¿Qué dices?

RICARDO (*Con angustia*)

¡Oh! No sé. No sé lo que digo.

---

[45] *No he querido ofenderle* I didn't mean to offend you

[46] *De tipo ... quisieran muchos* You are not at all a bad looking fellow in face or figure. There are many who would envy you

MARCELO

Usted no sabe lo que dice. Pero yo sí sé lo que está pensando ... A usted le resulta cómica esta hipótesis sencillamente porque yo soy un pobre hombre. ¡Sí! Un humilde profesor de francés desaliñado, torpe y tímido que pasa inadvertido en todas partes y a quien usted apenas saluda cuando le encuentra todas las mañanas en el vestíbulo 5 de esta casa. En una palabra: yo le parezco a usted muy poca cosa para amante de su mujer.[47]

RICARDO (*Dignamente*)

¡Señor mío! Tratándose de mi mujer[48] tengo derecho a desear para ella lo mejor.

CÁNDIDA (*Entre los dos, muy conciliadora*)

Pero si yo no soy nada exigente ... 10

RICARDO (*Un grito*)

¡Cándida!

CÁNDIDA

¡Ay Dios mío!

MARCELO

¡Sí! Le parezco a usted muy poco. Pero no porque usted crea que todo es poco para una mujer como la suya. ¡No! Es su enorme vanidad la que se ofende. Usted no puede concebir, ni siquiera con 15 la imaginación, que su rival sea un hombre tan modesto como yo ... Pues se equivoca usted, señor mío. Estoy en perfectas condiciones para ser el amante de su esposa.

RICARDO (*Airado*)

¿Está usted seguro?

---

[47] *yo le parezco ... su mujer* I seem to you a poor excuse as a candidate for your wife's lover

[48] *Tratándose de mi mujer* In matters concerning my wife

MARCELO

¡Sí! (*Vuelve los ojos hacia* CÁNDIDA *y la envuelve en una mirada emocionada.*[49] *Habla con otra voz, llena de la mayor ternura.*) ¿Cómo no voy a estarlo, si ella es mi vida y todos mis sueños?[50]

CÁNDIDA Y RICARDO (*Al tiempo*)

¿Qué?

MARCELO

5 ¡Señora! Ya no puedo callar más. Desde hace un año estoy enamorado de usted como un loco ... (CÁNDIDA *y* RICARDO, *sobresaltadísimos, se ponen en pie nuevamente.*)

RICARDO

¿Qué?

CÁNDIDA

¡Marcelo!

RICARDO (*Como un energúmeno*)

10 ¿Qué ha dicho? ... ¡Repítalo, que le mato![51]

CÁNDIDA (*Casi sin voz*)

Pero, Dios mío, ¿de verdad está usted enamorado de mí?

MARCELO (*Muy emocionado*)

¡Con toda mi alma! (CÁNDIDA, *conmovidísima, corre a* MARCELO *con las manos extendidas.*)

CÁNDIDA

¡Mi querido Marcelo!

---

[49] *la envuelve ... emocionada* he looks at her with deep affection
[50] *¿Cómo no ... mis sueños?* How could it be otherwise when she constitutes my life and all my dreams?
[51] *¡Repítalo, que le mato!* Repeat it, and I'll kill you!

MARCELO (*Emocionadísimo, cogiéndole las manos*)

¡Señora!

RICARDO (*Boquiabierto*)

Pero, Cándida ...

CÁNDIDA

¿No me engaña usted?

MARCELO

¡No! ¡Se lo juro!

CÁNDIDA (*Muy risueña*)

Pero, hombre, ¿por qué no me lo ha dicho usted antes? 5

RICARDO (*En un grito*)

¡¡Cándida!!

CÁNDIDA

¡Ricardo!

RICARDO

¿Es que te has vuelto loca?[52] ¡Ven aquí! (CÁNDIDA, *muy enfadada, se vuelve hacia* RICARDO.)

CÁNDIDA

Mi querido Ricardo. No estoy dispuesta a que me estropees este 10
momento.[53] Es la primera vez que se me declaran desde que tú me pediste relaciones hace veinte años, y la verdad que no me lo quiero perder ...[54]

---

[52] *¿Es que te has vuelto loca?* Have you lost your mind?
[53] *No estoy ... momento* I'm not willing to let you spoil this moment for me
[54] *y la verdad ... perder* and in all truth I don't want to miss this (opportunity)

RICARDO

Pero Cándida, Cándida. ¡Oh! (*Va de un lado a otro,*[55] *furiosísimo.* CÁNDIDA *va a* MARCELO *y, suavemente, con mucha ternura, le sienta en el sofá.*)

CÁNDIDA

Venga usted aquí, Marcelo. Póngase cómodo. ¿Un poco de
5 "whisky"?

MARCELO

Gracias. Lo necesito ...

CÁNDIDA

¿Dice usted que me quiere desde hace un año?

MARCELO (*Soñador*)

Justo. Desde el día que vine a esta casa para dar mi primera lección a Maité ... Llevaba usted un vestido azul con un gran cuello blanco.
10 No he podido olvidar ese vestido.

CÁNDIDA

¡Me lo pondré mañana!

MARCELO

¿De veras? ¿Hará usted eso por mí?

CÁNDIDA

Lo haré ... Es lo menos que usted se merece. ¿Ha sufrido usted mucho desde entonces?

MARCELO

15 Muchísimo.

[55] *Va de un lado a otro* He paces back and forth

CÁNDIDA (*Enternecida*)

Pobrecito, pobrecito mío. (RICARDO, *desde el fondo, furiosísimo, pega un puñetazo en cualquier parte.*)

RICARDO

¡Cándida! ¿Qué significa esto? ¿Qué te propones?[56] Dile a ese hombre que salga de mi casa ... ¡Díselo!

CÁNDIDA (*Muy enérgica*)

¡Ricardo! Esas voces son de muy mala educación ... [57] Y no sé por qué vas de un lado para otro como si estuvieras en una jaula. ¿Quieres decirme qué sucede para que te pongas así?[58] 5

RICARDO

Yo me voy a poner enfermo. Me siento muy mal ... Tengo fiebre.

CÁNDIDA

No tienes nada.[59] Estoy segura. ¿Quieres sentarte, sí o no?

RICARDO (*Desolado*)

Pero, Cándida. ¡Tú! ¡Tú! (*Está angustiadísimo. Ella le señala un sillón muy lejano.*) 10

CÁNDIDA

¡Siéntate ahí! Seamos sensatos, Ricardo. Marcelo se me ha declarado. Yo debo de estarle muy agradecida ...

RICARDO

¿Tú?

---

[56] *¿Qué te propones?* What do you intend (propose) to do?
[57] *Esas voces ... educación* That shouting shows very bad manners
[58] *¿Quieres decirme ... pongas así?* Will you please tell me why you are acting like this?
[59] *No tienes nada* There's nothing wrong with you

CÁNDIDA

¡Naturalmente! Una declaración de amor es siempre un homenaje. En principio, cuando un hombre se declara a una mujer, ella debe quedarle muy agradecida. Y en esta ocasión, tú, que eres mi marido, también debes estar muy agradecido a Marcelo ...

RICARDO

5 ¿Yo? ¡Es el colmo!

CÁNDIDA

Sí, tú. Parece mentira que un hombre de mundo como tú ignore estas cosas. Lo que pasa es que no estás en situación.[60] Te pones a dar gritos y paseos de un lado para otro y todavía no le has dado las gracias a monsieur Duval ...

RICARDO

10 ¡Cándida! ¿De verdad quieres que le dé las gracias?

CÁNDIDA

¡Sí!

MARCELO

Deje, deje ... (*Amablemente*) No se moleste.

CÁNDIDA

Por lo menos, siéntate y escucha ... Debemos oir a Marcelo. (*Sonríe. Le mira con cariño.*) Seguramente, tiene muchas cosas que 15 decirme.

MARCELO

"Oh madame! Ça m'ennuye beaucoup que votre mari soit ici ..."[61]

---

[60] *Lo que pasa ... situación* The trouble is you don't appreciate (understand) the situation

[61] "*Oh madame! ... soit ici*" (French) Oh madame! It annoys me to have your husband here

CÁNDIDA (*Confidencial*)

"Mais oui, cher Marcel. Je ne peux pas l'éviter."[62]

RICARDO (*Furioso*)

¡No!

CÁNDIDA

¡Oh!

RICARDO

¡En francés, no!

CÁNDIDA

¿Por qué? 5

RICARDO

¡Porque no lo entiendo!

CÁNDIDA (*Sublime*)

¡Qué egoísta eres! (*Transición. A* MARCELO, *piadosamente*) ¡Querido! Mi marido no sabe francés. A pesar de su emoción, ¿podrá usted hablarme en castellano?

MARCELO

Lo procuraré ... (*La mira a los ojos, sonríe. Baja los ojos ruborizado.* 10 *Habla con una indudable y honda verdad, emocionado.*) ¡Señora! El amor no tiene más que una frase sincera que tiene el mismo valor en todos los idiomas ... Una frase de dos palabras pequeñitas. ¡Te quiero!

RICARDO (*Superior*)

¡Oh! ¡De la vieja escuela![63]

MARCELO

¡Señora! ¡Dígale que no me interrumpa! 15

---

[62] "*Mais oui ... l'éviter*" (French) Of course, my dear Marcel. But I can't prevent it

[63] ¡ *De la vieja escuela*! He's of the old-fashioned school!

CÁNDIDA

¿Te quieres callar, sí o no? (*Dulcemente*) Siga, Marcelo. Decía usted: "Te quiero ... "

MARCELO

¡Señora! Desde hace un año tengo todos los días un momento de felicidad. Cuando usted entra por las mañanas en el cuarto de estudio
5 y me pregunta: "¿Cómo va Maité, profesor?"[64] Yo le contesto: "Muy mal, madame." Usted, entonces, se ríe, me tiende esa mano, que yo beso, y se va ... Sólo por esos instantes, que a veces duran unos pocos segundos, vivo desde hace un año.[65] Los domingos soy muy desgraciado porque no hay clase. Duermo soñando con usted.
10 Ando horas y horas por esas calles pensando en usted. Soy muy feliz por usted, y soy muy desgraciado por su culpa. A veces creo que la vida es alegre y bella como un jardín por la mañana. Otros días pienso que no merece la pena vivir. Así la quiero.[66] Durante estos últimos días la he tenido junto a mí con su perfume, con su mara-
15 villosa presencia, pero no he tenido fuerzas para cogerle una mano, para decirle un piropo, para rozar sus vestidos. ¿Comprende usted ahora mi timidez? Usted iba conmigo como en un juego. Yo iba con usted como en un sueño. Y ya ve usted, aunque todo era un juego, yo ¡pobre de mí! estaba jugando con esta verdad tan honda ... (*Se*
20 *calla. Sonríe.*) Bueno. Ya he hablado demasiado. En el amor sólo importan las dos palabras maravillosas: ¡Te quiero!

CÁNDIDA (*Muy bajo*)

Marcelo ... (*Un silencio. Ella, con disimulo, se seca una lágrima. Se levanta. Avanza.* MARCELO *sigue quieto en el sofá.* RICARDO, *alejado, en su sillón, mira al techo.*) Ha sido una declaración muy hermosa ...

RICARDO (*Un poco impresionado también*)

25 ¿Tú crees?

---

[64] "*¿Cómo va Maité, profesor?*" How is Maité doing, professor?
[65] *Sólo por esos instantes ... vivo desde hace un año* For the past year I have been living only for those moments, which sometimes last only a few seconds
[66] *Otros días ... la quiero* Other days I feel that life is not worth living. That is how I love you

CÁNDIDA

A ti, Ricardo, que tienes tanta costumbre, ¿qué te ha parecido?[67]

RICARDO

Mujer, yo ...

CÁNDIDA

Porque tú te has declarado a muchas señoras casadas.

RICARDO

Bueno, bueno ... Tanto como a muchas.[68] No exageres.

CÁNDIDA

Sí, a muchas. Y con éxito. ¡No seas modesto! 5

RICARDO

Bien, bien. Si lo que quieres de mí es una opinión técnica sobre la declaración de este caballero ...

CÁNDIDA

Eso mismo.

RICARDO

Entonces ... No tengo inconveniente. (*Se pone en pie, se estira los puños de la camisa y pregunta muy cortés.*) ¿Puedo hablar con sinceridad? 10 ¿No se ofenderá usted?

MARCELO (*Alarmado*)

¿Es que no le ha gustado?[69]

RICARDO

Pues, francamente ... , ¡no!

---

[67] *A ti ... ¿qué te ha parecido?* You're quite used to this sort of thing, Richard. What did you think of it?

[68] *Tanto como a muchas* I wouldn't say "many"

[69] *¿Es que no le ha gustado?* Do you mean that you didn't like it?

MARCELO

¡Oh! (*Dolidísimo*) Cómo lo siento ... Lo siento muchísimo. (MARCELO, *muy mohino, está en el sofá.* RICARDO *va hacia él, se sienta a su lado y le da unos consoladores golpecitos en la espalda.*)

RICARDO

¡Ea, ea! no hay que amilanarse.[70] No desespere. Lo que ocurre es
5 que tiene usted un concepto demasiado romántico del amor. No es eso, no es eso, amigo mío. Las mujeres gustan del amor rosa en las novelas, en las comedias y en el cine ... Pero en la vida prefieren el amor un poco más audaz. Se ha declarado usted a mi mujer como podría haberle pedido relaciones a una colegiala un teniente de
10 infantería.[71] Ha hablado usted de sueños, de jardines ... ¡Ta, ta, ta! Vieja escuela, querido, vieja escuela. Tiene usted mucho que aprender. Las casadas no se rinden así. ¿Me permite usted que le haga una demostración práctica?[72] Figúrese usted que mi mujer no es mi mujer, sino una mujer casada a la que yo hago esta noche el
15 amor ... (*Se pone en pie y va hacia* CÁNDIDA.) ¡Cándida! Te quiero. Te he querido siempre a ti sola. Tú eres toda mi vida. ¡No juegues conmigo, Cándida, no juegues! Te quiero. ¡Te quiero tanto! (*La mira hondamente.*[73] *La coge entre sus brazos. La besa. Es un beso profundo, apasionado.*)

MARCELO

20 ¡Oh! ¡Oh!

CÁNDIDA

¡Ricardo! Cómo puedes ... (*Se retira, avergonzada, y se sienta en un sillón.* RICARDO, *muy ufano, se vuelve hacia* MARCELO.)

RICARDO

¿Qué? ¿Ha visto usted?

---

[70] *¡Ea, ea!, no hay que amilanarse* Come, come! One mustn't be discouraged

[71] *como podría ... infantería* just as a young "cadet" would have proposed to a school girl (since "inexperience" is implied, the literal translation of "lieutenant" would not have quite the same meaning)

[72] *¿Me permite ... práctica?* Will you let me give you a practical demonstration?

[73] *La mira hondamente* He looks deep into her eyes

MARCELO

Sí.

RICARDO

¿Qué le parece?

MARCELO (*Con tímida rabia*)

¡Me parece un abuso![74]

RICARDO (*Riendo*)

¡Naturalmente! Pero, amigo mío, ¿todavía no sabe usted que el amor es un continuo abuso de confianza?[75] (*Muy risueño*) Y tú, querida, ¿qué opinas? Quién tiene razón, ¿él o yo? (*Un silencio.* CÁNDIDA *calla, mira a uno y a otro. Al fin, baja los ojos al suelo.*) 5

CÁNDIDA

¡Él!

RICARDO

¿Qué?

CÁNDIDA

Él tiene razón porque dice la verdad. ¡Habla con el corazón! Tú, no. Tú, mientes. 10

RICARDO

¡Cándida!

CÁNDIDA

¡Sí! Mientes siempre. Tus palabras son mentira. Tus besos son mentira. ¡Todo es mentira!

---

[74] *¡Me parece un abuso!* I think you took advantage of her trust! (the word *abuso* here means "deception" rather than "abuse")

[75] *¿todavía ... de confianza?* Don't you know yet that love always means taking advantage of the other person's trust?

RICARDO (*Estupefacto*)

¡Cándida! ¿Qué juego es éste? (*Un silencio. Al fin,* MARCELO *avanza hacia* CÁNDIDA *y le besa una mano que ella le tiende.*)

MARCELO

Gracias, madame … (*Un silencio*) ¿Puedo retirarme?

CÁNDIDA

Sí, Marcelo. Yo le acompaño.[76] Buenas noches.

5 (*Salen los dos.* RICARDO, *solo en primer término, en un sillón, hunde la cabeza entre las manos. Por una puerta lateral asoman con muchísima cautela* MAITÉ, MANOLÍN *y* TONY. *Los tres visten ya pijama. Cuchichean en la entrada.*)

MAITÉ

¡Chiss!

TONY

10 ¿Qué habrá pasado?[77]

MAITÉ

No lo sé. Pero ha debido de ser horrible …

MANOLÍN

No veo nada roto …

MAITÉ

¡Oh! Mirad. ¡El marido! (*Los tres avanzan hacia* RICARDO, *mirándole piadosamente.*)

TONY

15 ¡Papá! ¿Le … le has pegado?

[76] *Yo le acompaño* I'll see you to the door
[77] *¿Qué habrá pasado?* I wonder what happened?

RICARDO

¿Yo? No.

MANOLÍN (*Asustado*)

¿Es que te ha pegado él a ti?

RICARDO

No ... Tampoco.

MAITÉ (*Con evidente disgusto*)

Pues no me lo explico, porque estaba todo a punto. Lo que pasa es que la gente no se pega por nada ... [78] Ya se ve. (RICARDO *alza la cabeza y los contempla irritado.*) 5

RICARDO

¿Qué estáis diciendo? ¿Qué hacéis aquí vosotros?

LOS TRES MUCHACHOS (*Con susto*)

¡Ay!

(*Los tres chicos, llenos de pavor, desaparecen corriendo.* RICARDO *se hunde de nuevo en el sillón. Una levísima pausa. Entra* CÁNDIDA. *Muy despacio, se sienta en el sofá, lejos de* RICARDO.) 10

RICARDO

Ni una palabra, ¿sabes? No quiero que hablemos ni una palabra sobre este absurdo incidente ...

CÁNDIDA

Mejor será ... [79]

---

[78] *porque estaba ... por nada* because everything was set just right. The trouble is that people absolutely refuse to fight

[79] *Mejor será ...* It's just as well

RICARDO (*La mira. Un silencio. Una transición*)

Oye ... ¿Qué te parecería si tú y yo, solos, hiciésemos un viaje a Mallorca?[80] ¿Eh?

CÁNDIDA

¿A Mallorca? (*Sorprendida*) Pero si ya hemos estado en Mallorca ...

RICARDO

¡Por eso!

CÁNDIDA

5 No, no. Es absurdo volver a los sitios donde ya se ha estado ... Todo el mundo dice que ha cambiado mucho, pero no es verdad. Lo único que pasa es que han puesto trolebuses.[81] Y, la verdad, no merece la pena ir a Palma para ver si han puesto trolebuses ...

RICARDO

Es que me gustaría volver a vivir todo aquello. Me gustaría volver a 10 comprarte en Manacor un collar de perlas, como entonces. Me gustaría volver a visitar contigo las cuevas del Drach, una mañana de domingo, para oir el concierto de Chopin[82] que tocan los músicos en la barca llena de luces ... ¿Recuerdas? Yo, en el fondo, soy un sentimental.

CÁNDIDA

15 ¡Ah! Era por eso ...

RICARDO

Sí, Cándida. Quisiera volver a empezar. Si tú quieres ... Sería tan sencillo y tan bonito. Mi vida desde mañana va a cambiar por completo. Seré otro hombre: el que he debido de ser siempre.[83] Ya verás, ya verás ... Voy a ser un auténtico padre de familia. No 20 comeré fuera. No saldré de noche. Tú y yo siempre juntos ...

---

[80] *Mallorca:* (See vocabulary for place references)

[81] *Lo único ... trolebuses* The only change is that they have installed trolley buses

[82] *Chopin:* 19th century Polish pianist and composer of great fame. He lived in Mallorca for some time because of his failing health

[83] *el que ... siempre* the one I should always have been

CÁNDIDA

¿Qué dices, Ricardo?

RICARDO

Lo que oyes. ¡Voy a cambiar de vida!

CÁNDIDA (*Indignada*)

¡Ah, no! Eso sí que no ... [84] De manera que te has pasado veinte años de matrimonio divirtiéndote a tu gusto y esta noche, precisamente esta noche, quieres cambiar de vida. (*Muy enfadada*) ¡Ricardo! 5
Nunca creí que fueras tan egoísta.

RICARDO (*Atónito*)

¿Qué dices?

CÁNDIDA

Además, es imposible. Tú eres como eres y serías muy desgraciado si fueras de otro modo. Te pondrías enfermo. Lo sé. A los trasnochadores como tú les sienta muy mal quedarse en casa ... [85] Se 10
acatarran. (*Sonríe.*) No, Ricardo. No es necesario que tomes actitudes heroicas. Mira, esta noche, sentada en ese sofá entre Marcelo y tú, he comprendido muchas cosas. ¡Muchísimas! Tantas, que, en un minuto, te he comprendido a ti, y al comprenderte te he perdonado tus veinte años de infidelidades. Tú no me has engañado por frivo- 15
lidad, ni siquiera por capricho, mi pobre Ricardo. Has sido un marido infiel porque no has tenido más remedio que serlo.[86] Porque el peligro te atraía y tiraba de ti y jugaba con tu voluntad. Es maravillosa esa fascinación de lo peligroso ... Bien lo sé ahora. Esta noche acabo de oir palabras de amor de otro hombre que no eras tú. 20
Y sé que me ha gustado oirlas ... (*Sonríe.*) Ya ves, ahora no podría juzgarte mal, querido Ricardo. He descubierto que a mí también me atrae el peligro ... No debe extrañarte. Después de todo, yo también soy un ser humano como tú.

[84] *Eso sí que no* No, I won't have it!
[85] *A los trasnochadores ... casa* Staying at home doesn't agree with night owls like you
[86] *no has tenido ... serlo* you couldn't help yourself

RICARDO

Me asusta oirte. No sé qué quieres decir ...

CÁNDIDA (*Sonríe*)

Nada ... (*Se ríe.*) No te preocupes demasiado. La verdad es que la vida es casi una broma. Eso también lo he aprendido esta noche. Un juego de personas mayores que a veces puede empezar como un
5 juego de niños.
(*Entra* ROSITA.)

ROSITA

¡Señora! Monsieur Duval llama a la señora por teléfono ... (*Y sale.*)

CÁNDIDA

¡Ah! Sí ... Dijo que llamaría desde el café de la esquina. (*Corre al teléfono. Toma el auricular de la mesita. Cuando va a hablar, piensa, sonríe*
10 *y lo vuelve a dejar en su sitio.*) Bueno; si no te importa, hablaré desde mi cuarto ... Es más cómodo.

RICARDO

Sí, claro ...

CÁNDIDA

Buenas noches, Ricardo. Hasta mañana.

RICARDO

Buenas noches.
15 (CÁNDIDA *sale aprisa por una puerta de la derecha. La primera intención de* RICARDO, *solo, es escuchar. Coge el auricular. Pero se arrepiente y lo suelta rápido. Luego, abatido, ensimismado, marcha hacia el fondo. Apaga las luces. Entra en la terraza. Se le ve allá entre las sombras,*[87] *apoyado inmóvil en el antepecho. La escena ha quedado casi a oscuras, sin más luz que el*
20 *resplandor de la luna que entra por la terraza. Surgen, como tres duendes,* MAITÉ, MANOLÍN *y* TONY. *Cada uno de los tres, a sus anchas, va fumando un cigarrillo.*)

[87] *Se le ve ... sombras* He is seen there in the shadows

MANOLÍN (*Un cuchicheo*)

¿Qué?

TONY

Nadie ...

MAITÉ

¡Chist! (MAITÉ *avanza hacia la puerta por donde desapareció* CÁNDIDA. *Los otros la siguen.* MAITÉ *escucha.*)

TONY

¿Están ahí? 5

MAITÉ

!Sí! Están los dos. Al tío Ricardo no se le oye.[88] Pero tía Cándida no hace más que decirle:[89] "Es maravilloso, maravilloso ... "

TONY

¡Bravo!

MAITÉ (*Muy bajito, satisfechísima*)

¡Ay, la verdad es que hemos tenido una buena idea! Esta noche ya podemos dormir tranquilos ... ¡Chist! (*Marchan de puntillas.*) 10

TELÓN

---

[88] *Al tío Ricardo no se le oye* You can't hear Uncle Richard
[89] *Pero tía Cándida no hace más que decirle* But Aunt Cándida merely keeps repeating

Acto Tercero

El mismo decorado. A la mañana siguiente del acto anterior. MAITÉ, sentada a la mesa, desayuna. Mientras come, lee atentísimamente un ejemplar de *ABC*.[1] ROSITA, al otro extremo de la escena, ordena, en un cacharro, un ramo de flores.

ROSITA

5 ¡Señorita! ¿Se puede saber qué lee usted con tanto interés? ¡Es que hay algún crimen bueno?

MAITÉ

¡Ay, no! Estoy leyendo los "Ecos de sociedad."[2]

ROSITA

¡Ah! ¿Sí?

MAITÉ (*Felicísima*)

¡Huy! Me chiflan ... Mira. Hay unas cuantas personas importantes
10 que van a todas las fiestas, y claro, salen todos los días en los "Ecos de sociedad" de *ABC*. Como siempre son los mismos, yo ya me los sé de memoria. Y les he tomado mucho cariño ...[3] Vamos, los quiero como si fueran amigos íntimos.

---

1 ABC: Daily news magazine founded in 1905 by Torcuato Luca de Tena
2 "*Ecos de sociedad*": The Society Section of *ABC*
3 *Y les he tomado mucho cariño* And I've become very fond of them

ROSITA

¡No me diga!

MAITÉ

Ya lo creo. Cuando hay una fiesta y alguno de los que van siempre no aparece en *ABC*, me cuesta un disgusto.[4] Ahora mismo, la duquesa de Monteviejo me tiene muy preocupada. Se ha perdido tres "cockteles" y un té. 5

ROSITA

Eso es que[5] la duquesa se ha retirado a la vida privada.

MAITÉ

¡Ca! Eso es que ha pescado una gripe ...

ROSITA

¿Usted cree?

MAITÉ

¡Vamos! Si no es por enfermedad, esta duquesa no se pierde tres guateques así como así. ¡Si la conoceré yo![6] (*Transición*) Oye ... 10
¿Para dónde son esas flores?

ROSITA

Para el cuarto de estudio. La señora ha ordenado que, desde hoy, todas las mañanas haya flores en el cuarto cuando monsieur Duval dé su lección a la señorita ...

MAITÉ

¡Anda! 15

---

[4] *me cuesta un disgusto* it upsets me
[5] *Eso es que* It means that (*or* That's because)
[6] *no se pierde ... conoceré yo!* she isn't likely to miss three wild parties for no good reason. As if I didn't know her!

ROSITA

Sí, señorita. Y, además, la señora quiere que todos los días se sirva a monsieur Duval una taza de café y un "croissant." Dice la señora que hay que cuidar mucho al profesor, porque el pobrecito vive solo en una pensión y está muy abandonado ...

MAITÉ

5 ¡Ay! (*Regocijadísima*) De modo que flores en el estudio, café y un "croissant." ¡Es fantástico! Resulta que tía Cándida finge tan bien que parece que se ha enamorado de verdad de monsieur Duval ...

ROSITA

¡Toma! Como que hace un ratito, cuando la señora me daba estas órdenes y hablaba de monsieur Duval, le brillaban los ojos de una
10 manera ... Yo juraría que se le saltaban las lágrimas.[7]

MAITÉ

¡Fabuloso! Nadie hubiera creído que tía Cándida era capaz de representar una comedia de ese modo. Para que se fíe una de las señoras que no han roto un plato ... [8]

(*Entra* MANOLÍN. *Se lanza, casi con desesperación, a ocupar un puesto en*
15 *la mesa. Durante las primeras palabras de la escena que sigue,* ROSITA *abandona el arreglo del búcaro y entra en la terraza, donde se ocupa en arreglar las plantas. Luego desaparece por la izquierda de la terraza. Quedan solos en escena* MAITÉ *y* MANOLÍN.

MANOLÍN

¡Pronto! Mi desayuno ....

MAITÉ

20 Hola, hombre. ¿Qué vas a tomar?

---

7 *se le saltaban las lágrimas* she was on the verge of tears

8 *Para que ... un plato* One can't trust these ladies who look so innocent (*literally*, who have never broken a plate)

MANOLÍN

De todo ... Café, mermelada, mantequilla y pan. ¡Mucho pan!

MAITÉ

¡Ay hijo! ¡Qué apetito más ordinario!

MANOLÍN (*Comiendo*)

Es que me muero de hambre ... No sé qué me pasa por las mañanas ...

MAITÉ

Lo mismo que a todas horas ...[9] ¡Que te pasas el día comiendo!

MANOLÍN (*Con la boca llena*)

¿Tú crees? 5

MAITÉ

Claro que sí. Pero no te preocupes, hijo. (*Muy suficiente*) Cuando seas mayor y te enamores perderás el apetito. Ya verás, pequeño, ya verás ... (MANOLÍN *se pone en pie lleno de furia.*)

MANOLÍN

¡¡Maité!!

MAITÉ (*Muy asustada*)

¡Ay! 10

MANOLÍN

¡Si me vuelves a llamar pequeño otra vez, te atizo!

MAITÉ (*Con mucha dignidad*)

¿A mí? ¿A una señorita?

MANOLÍN

¡Sí, a ti! ¿Qué pasa?

---

[9] *Lo mismo ... horas* The same that's always wrong with you

MAITÉ

¡Salvaje! ¡Ordinario! ¡Bruto! ¡Más que bruto!

MANOLÍN

¡Ea! que ya estoy muy harto. Tanto pequeño por aquí y pequeño por allá.[10] ¡Porras!

MAITÉ

¡Bruto! ¡Bruto! ¡Bruto!

5 (*Aparece* TONY. *Viene listo para salir a la calle. De punta en blanco,*[11] *elegantísimo*)

TONY

¡Chist! ¿Hay bronca? (MAITÉ *y* MANOLÍN *se vuelven hacia el recién llegado y de pronto olvidan su pendencia, porque se quedan suspensos viendo el elegante porte de* TONY.)

MAITÉ

10 ¡Tony!

MANOLÍN

¡Chico!

MAITÉ

¡Qué elegancia!

TONY

Psché … ¿De verdad estoy bien?[12] ¿Os gusto?

MANOLÍN

¡Toma! Si hasta se ha puesto una corbata de papá …

---

[10] *¡Ea! que ya … por allá* All right! I'm fed up with being called "little one" by everyone!

[11] *De punta en blanco* All decked out (*or* All dressed up)

[12] *¿De verdad estoy bien?* Do I really look all right?

MAITÉ

Oye. ¿Y se puede saber adónde vas tú tan peripuesto y tan de mañana?

TONY (*Misterioso*)

¡Psché! Cosas.

MAITÉ

¿Cosas? Oye, oye, oye ...

TONY

¡Je! (*Tímidamente*) Verás ... Es que tengo una cita. 5

MAITÉ

¿Una cita? ¿Dónde?

TONY

¡Je! ¡En el Retiro! En la Rosaleda ...

MAITÉ (*Interesadísima*)

¿Con quién?

TONY

Pues ... (*Heroicamente*) Con Piluca Montes.

MAITÉ (*Escamadísima*)

¡Ah! ¿Sí? ¿Y por qué te has citado con Piluca Montes en la Rosaleda? 10

TONY

Bueno. Es que anoche no tuve tiempo de decírtelo. Como estábamos tan ocupados arreglando los conflictos de mamá ... Pero ayer me encontré a Piluca y se me declaró ...[13]

---

[13] *se me declaró* she proposed (*or* she asked me to go steady with her)

MAITÉ (*Casi en un grito*)

¿Qué?

TONY

Sí. Y quedamos en vernos hoy por la mañana en la Rosaleda para que yo le dijera lo que había decidido. ¿Comprendes?

MAITÉ (*Excitadísima*)

Entonces es que Piluca Montes te ha puesto los puntos ...[14]

TONY

5 Sí, sí. ¡Y de qué manera, chica![15]

MAITÉ

La muy ...

TONY Y MANOLÍN (*Asustadísimos*)

¡Maité!

MAITÉ

La muy ...

MANOLÍN

Oye, tú. A ver si dices algo que no podamos oir nosotros ...[16]

MAITÉ (*Al fin*)

10 ¡La muy ... fresca, descarada, sinvergüenza!

TONY

¡Maité!

---

[14] *Entonces ... los puntos* The fact is, then, that Piluca Montes has made things (*i.e.*, her feelings) quite plain to you

[15] *Sí, sí. ¡ Y de qué manera, chica!* She certainly has ... and how!

[16] *A ver si ... nosotros* Watch out you don't say something we're not supposed to hear

MAITÉ

¡La arranco el pelo![17] (*Con muchísimo coraje*) Esa pécora ... Esa coqueta ... Esa mala amiga. De manera que se te ha declarado sabiendo lo que sabe, porque yo le he hecho confidencias y se lo he contado todo ...

TONY (*En la luna*)

¡Anda! Y ¿qué es lo que sabe? 5

MAITÉ (*Enrojeciendo*)

¿A ti qué te importa?[18] (*Transición. Irritadísima*) ¡Tony! Quítate ese traje y devuélvele esa corbata al tío Ricardo, porque tú no vas hoy a la Rosaleda ...

TONY (*Muy contrariado*)

Pero, mujer ...

MAITÉ

¡He dicho que no vas! ¿Me has oído? 10

TONY

¡Y dale! (*Mohino*) ¡Siempre que voy a tener novia te pones tú en medio! Ya me has estropeado tres proporciones ...[19]

MAITÉ

Y te estropearé otras tres. Y muchas más. ¡Pues no faltaría otra cosa![20]

---

[17] ¡*La arranco el pelo*! I'll pull her hair out! (*coll.* use of *la* for *le*)
[18] ¿*A ti qué te importa*? That doesn't concern you!
[19] ¡*Y dale*! ... *tres proporciones* There you go again! Whenever I'm going to have a girl friend you always get in the way! You've already ruined for me three possibilities
[20] ! *Pues no faltaría otra cosa*! Why, the very idea! Why shouldn't I?

TONY (*Indignado débilmente*)

Pero ¿es que yo no tengo derecho a tener novia?

MAITÉ

¡Claro que sí! Y la tendrás.[21] Pero no esa lagartona de Piluca, ni otras por el estilo ... Tú tendrás la novia que te mereces. La única que debes tener. ¿Comprendes? La que más te quiere ...

TONY (*Curiosísimo*)

5 Oye ... Y ¿quién es esa?

MAITÉ

¿Esa? (*Enrojece, se azara muchísimo.*) Pues quién va a ser ...[22]

TONY

¿La conoces tú?

MAITÉ (*Se va a echar a llorar*)

¡Huy! Muchísimo. Una barbaridad ... ¡Ay Dios mío! Pero qué tonto, retonto, que tontísimo eres.

TONY (*Estupefacto*)

10 ¡Maité!

MANOLÍN

¡Chica!

MAITÉ (*Azaradísima, llorando con verdadero desconsuelo*)

¡Ay Dios mío! ¡Qué desgraciada soy! Pero ¡qué desgraciada! ... (*Y toda llena de rubores escapa corriendo por el fondo.* TONY *y* MANOLÍN *se quedan estupefactos mirándose de hito en hito.*)[23]

---

[21] *Y la tendrás* And you will have one
[22] *Pues quién va a ser* Well, who else can it be
[23] *mirándose de hito en hito* staring at each other

TONY

¿Has oído?

MANOLÍN

¡Sí!

TONY (*Emocionadísimo*)

¿Si será ...?[24]

MANOLÍN

Yo creo que sí ...

TONY

¿Si será ...? ¿Si será ...? (*Transportado por el júbilo y la sorpresa escapa hacia el fondo.*) ¡Maité, escucha! ... ¡Espera, Maité! 5

MANOLÍN (*Muy contento*)

¡Chico!

(*Y sale también* MANOLÍN *corriendo detrás de su hermano. Un segundo la escena sola. Entra* RICARDO. *Tiene un gesto huraño, un humor pésimo. Va a la mesita, se sienta y, maquinalmente, comienza a desayunar. Un instante* 10 *después regresa a escena* ROSITA, *por la terraza. Se dirige al lugar donde está el búcaro de flores que antes compuso, lo toma y se dispone a salir.*)

ROSITA

Buenos días. ¿Necesita algo el señor?

RICARDO

¡No! (*Transición*) Un momento. ¿Adónde vas con esas flores?

ROSITA (*Sonríe*)

Son para la mesa de monsieur Duval ... 15

[24] *¿ Si será ... ?* I wonder if it could be ... ?

RICARDO

¡Oh! (*Nerviosamente, se le cae una cucharilla, que hace un ruido tremendo.* ROSITA *inquiere amablemente.*)

ROSITA

¿Le sucede algo al señor?

RICARDO (*Ceñudo*)

¡Vete! Déjame en paz ...

ROSITA

5 Sí, señor ...

(*Sale* ROSITA *con sus flores.* RICARDO *toma su café. Aparece* CÁNDIDA. *Viste un bonito traje azul con un gran cuello blanco.* RICARDO, *al verla, se pone en pie, casi de un brinco.*)[25]

RICARDO

¡Cándida!

CÁNDIDA

10 ¡Ay! ¿Qué?

RICARDO

¡Ese vestido! ¡Has sido capaz de ponerte ese vestido![26]

CÁNDIDA (*Sonríe*)

Naturalmente ... ¿Ya no recuerdas que se lo prometí anoche a Marcelo? Yo llevaba este vestido cuando él me conoció, hace un año,[27] y se enamoró de mí. Para él es un bello recuerdo. ¿Qué
15 quieres? Me parece de muy buen gusto que hoy vuelva a encontrarme tal como me vio entonces ...

[25] *se pone ... brinco* he almost jumps to his feet
[26] ¡ *Has sido ... vestido*! You actually had the nerve to wear that dress!
[27] *cuando ... hace un año* when he met me a year ago

RICARDO

Eso no es decente ...

CÁNDIDA

¿Qué dices? Si es un modelo recatadísimo ...

RICARDO

¡Está pasado de moda!

CÁNDIDA (*Sonríe*)

No ... Los recuerdos no pasan de moda. (*Se sienta a la mesa y se prepara el desayuno. Habla con una alegre ternura.*) ¡Pobrecillo Marcelo! Quién iba a pensar[28] que en un hombre tan tímido y tan delicado había un ser tan apasionado. Ha sido una deliciosa sorpresa. Claro que yo comprendo que a ti no te puede resultar simpático.[29] ¡Sois tan diferentes! En él todo es quietud y serenidad y paz ... Tú eres el alboroto, el ruido, el escándalo. Como si dijéramos: Marcelo es el ideal para marido, y en cambio tú eres el perfecto amante. (*Suspira.*) Lo malo es cuando una se casa con el amante. Entonces resulta que no tiene una ni amante ni marido ... (*Con volubilidad*) ¿Quieres otra taza de café?

RICARDO

¡No!

CÁNDIDA (*Con risueña impaciencia*)

Debe de estar al llegar.[30] Es la hora de su lección a Maité ... Verás cómo se emociona al verme. (*Sonríe.*) Dicen que los enamorados, cuando sueñan, recuerdan siempre a la amada tal como la vieron el primer día. (*Se mira y vuelve a sonreir.*) A mí eso me conviene, ¿sabes? Reconozco que este vestido me favorece un poco ... (*Transición*) Te costó dos mil pesetas.

[28] *Quién iba a pensar* Who would ever have thought

[29] *yo comprendo ... simpático* I realize that you can't be expected to find him attractive

[30] *Debe de estar al llegar* He should be here any moment

RICARDO (*Cejijunto*)

Dos mil quinientas.

CÁNDIDA

¿Tanto?

RICARDO

¡Sí! Esas cosas nunca se me olvidan ...

CÁNDIDA

Pues es caro ...

RICARDO

5 Eso dije yo entonces y tú te empeñaste en que era una ganga ...

CÁNDIDA

Sí, es posible. Pero, si lo piensas bien, verás que el tiempo me ha dado la razón.[31] Por unas pocas pesetas diste ocasión a despertar un gran amor en el corazón de Marcelo ... ¿No te sientes orgulloso?

RICARDO

Mucho ... Muchísimo. Es una verdadera satisfacción para un marido
10 haber contribuído con dos mil quinientas pesetas a que otro hombre se enamore de su mujer.

CÁNDIDA (*Amablemente*)

¿Quieres un poco más de café?

RICARDO (*Furioso*)

¡Te he dicho que no!

CÁNDIDA

¡Ay! Ricardo ..., ¿qué te sucede?

---

[31] *el tiempo ... razón* time has proved me right

RICARDO

¡Que voy a estallar![32] ¡Que me voy a volver loco! ¡Que voy a hacer un disparate! ¡Eso!

CÁNDIDA

¡Ricardo!

RICARDO

Pero Cándida, reflexiona, por favor. ¿Tú crees que puedo resignarme con el papel que me corresponde en todo lo que aquí está sucediendo desde anoche? 5

CÁNDIDA

¿Sabes lo que pienso?

RICARDO

¿Qué?

CÁNDIDA

Que otro, en tu lugar, estaría muy ufano ...

RICARDO

¡Cándida! 10

CÁNDIDA

Sí, no me mires así. Lo natural es que un marido se sienta halagado cuando su mujer es capaz de despertar todavía una gran pasión. Sobre todo un hombre de ideas morales tan audaces y tan modernas como las tuyas ... Lo que pasa es que tú eres muy moderno cuando tratas de conquistar a la mujer de un amigo. Pero, claro, cuando es 15 otro hombre el que le hace el amor a tu mujer, entonces pones el grito en el cielo ...[33] ¡Ah! No, hijo. Eso no vale.[34]

---

[32] ¡ *Que voy a estallar*! I'm going to explode! (The *que* is not translated in these constructions)

[33] *pones el grito en el cielo* you scream to high heaven

[34] *Eso no vale* That's not fair

RICARDO

¡Cándida! Me pareces otra. Jamás has hablado con esa frivolidad. ¿No te das cuenta de que todo esto es muy grave? Anoche, de madrugada, en esta misma habitación, en mi presencia, un hombre se ha declarado a mi mujer ...

CÁNDIDA

5 Bueno. Pero de una manera bastante original. Por primera vez, en escena había un francés y no era el marido ... Era el otro.[35]

RICARDO

Después, ese individuo te llamó por teléfono y estuvisteis hablando durante más de media hora. Y todavía no me has dicho ni una sola palabra de lo que contratasteis en esa conversación.

CÁNDIDA

10 ¡Naturalmente!

RICARDO

¿Por qué?

CÁNDIDA (*Sonríe. Despacito*)

Por discreción. Agradécemelo ...

RICARDO (*Furioso*)

¿Qué te dijo?

CÁNDIDA

Por Dios, Ricardo.

RICARDO (*Tozudo*)

15 ¿Qué te dijo?

---

[35] *Por primera vez ... el otro* For the first time a Frenchman was playing the role not of the (betrayed) husband, but the other role (*i.e.*, the lover) (a probable allusion to French farces)

CÁNDIDA

Vamos. No seas niño. Me dijo las cosas naturales que dice un enamorado. Figúrate todo lo que quieras. (*Sonríe.*) Lo gracioso es que por teléfono todo el mundo resulta más atrevido de lo que es en realidad. Y Marcelo ...

RICARDO

¿Qué? 5

CÁNDIDA

Estuvo atrevidísimo ... No quieras saber.

RICARDO

¿Te ... faltó al respeto?[36]

CÁNDIDA (*Encantada*)

Un poco ... Lo correcto.

RICARDO

¡Oh! ¡Lo mato![37]

CÁNDIDA

No digas barbaridades. En los crímenes pasionales, el personaje más antipático es el asesino ... 10

RICARDO (*Con cierta curiosidad*)

Oye ... ¿Te habló de mí?

CÁNDIDA

No quería decírtelo. Pero como te empeñas ... Me habló de ti ...

---

36 *¿Te ... faltó al respeto?* Was he disrespectful to you?

37 *¡Oh! ¡Lo mato!* Oh! I'll kill him! (The present tense replaces the future for emphasis)

RICARDO

¿Y qué?

CÁNDIDA (*Con el natural sentimiento*)

No le eres simpático ... No le gustas.[38]

RICARDO

¿Nada?

CÁNDIDA

¡Nada!

RICARDO

5 No me lo explico.

CÁNDIDA

Yo tampoco ... (*Alentadora*) Pero, en fin, confío en que, con el tiempo, os acostumbraréis el uno al otro.

RICARDO (*En un grito*)

¡Cándida!

CÁNDIDA

¡Ay!

RICARDO

10 ¿Qué has querido insinuar?

CÁNDIDA

Mi querido Ricardo ... (*Dignamente*) Si estás decidido a interpretar con un doble sentido[39] todo lo que yo diga, no seguiremos hablando.

---

[38] *No le eres ... gustas* You're not an attractive person to him ... He doesn't like you

[39] *Si estás decidido ... sentido* If you're determined to misinterpret

RICARDO (*Volviéndose hacia ella con violencia*)

Pero, ¿es que crees que no sé todo lo que ocurre dentro de ti en este momento? ¿Crees que no veo la enorme ilusión con que te has puesto ese estúpido vestido anticuado, y con qué coquetería te has pintado los labios, y te has peinado de otro modo, todo, todo para que cuando ese ... caballero entre por esa puerta te encuentre más bonita y más agradable que nunca? 5

CÁNDIDA

¡Ricardo! ¿De verdad se me nota mucho que me he arreglado un poco?[40]

RICARDO

¡Sí! Se nota una barbaridad ...[41] Es una vergüenza.

CÁNDIDA

¡Ah! Pues tendré que disimular ... No me gustaría que Marcelo me considerase demasiado fácil ... Sería horrible ... 10

RICARDO (*Desesperado*)

¡Cándida! ¿Es que sólo piensas en él?[42]

(*Se deja caer, abrumadísimo, en un sillón.* CÁNDIDA *está lejos, al otro lado. Entra* MAITÉ *corriendo, y con gran alborozo se dirige a su tía.*)

MAITÉ

¡Tía Cándida! (*Alegrísima*) ¡Ahí viene monsieur Duval! 15

CÁNDIDA (*Nerviosa*)

¡Ay! ¿Ya?

---

[40] *¿De verdad ... un poco?* Is it really so obvious that I'm somewhat dressed up?
[41] *¡Sí! Se nota una barbaridad* Yes! It's extremely obvious
[42] *¿Es que sólo piensas en él?* Can't you think of anyone but him?

MAITÉ

Le he visto cruzar la calle desde el balcón de mi cuarto ... ¿Te has arreglado bien?

CÁNDIDA

Yo creo que sí. ¿Qué te parece a ti?

MAITÉ

A ver, a ver ... (*Muy satisfecha del examen*) ¡Imponente! Estás
5 guapísima. No me extraña que le tengas chiflado ... [43]

RICARDO

¡Maité!

MAITÉ

¡Ay! ¿Qué?

RICARDO

¡Que estoy yo aquí!

MAITÉ (*Casi sin mirarle*)

¡Ah, bueno! Hola, tío. (*Transición, como ántes*) Dime, tía Cándida.
10 ¿Estás muy nerviosa?

CÁNDIDA

Pues sí, hija. Como desde que me casé no me habían vuelto a pasar estas cosas ...

(*Entra* TONY.)

TONY

¡Mamá! ¡Mamá! ¡Que viene monsieur Duval! ¡Y cómo viene! ¡Con
15 traje nuevo, no te digo más![44]

(*Entra velozmente* MANOLÍN.)

---

[43] *No me extraña ... chiflado* I'm not surprised that he has lost his head over you

[44] *¡ Y cómo viene! ... más!* You should see him! He's wearing a new suit! Need I say more?

MANOLÍN

¡Mamá! ¡Ahí está monsieur Duval! Y no sabéis lo bueno ... [45]

TODOS

¿Qué?

MANOLÍN

¡Se ha puesto una flor en la solapa!

TODOS

¡Oh!

MAITÉ (*Palmoteando*)

¡Es un sol! ¡Un sol! 5

RICARDO (*Horrorizado*)

¡Hay que ver! ¡Cómo se ha perdido la moral en esta casa![46]
(*Entra* ROSITA.)

ROSITA

¡Señora! (RICARDO *se yergue y casi pega un grito.*)

RICARDO

¡Sí!

TODOS (*Con susto*)

¡Ay! 10

RICARDO (*Furiosísimo*)

Dilo tú también. ¡Dilo! Ahí está monsieur Duval que quiere ver a la señora. ¿No es eso?

---

[45] *Y no sabéis lo bueno* And you don't know the best part yet
[46] *¡Hay que ver! ... esta casa!* It seems incredible! This house has lost all sense of morality!

ROSITA (*Tranquilamente*)

No, señor.

TODOS

¿Eh?

ROSITA

Monsieur Duval desea hablar a solas con el señor ...

RICARDO

¡Hola! (*Transición*) ¿Estás segura?

ROSITA

5 Sí, señor. Eso ha dicho.

RICARDO

¡Caramba, caramba! (*Encantado*) Resulta que a quien quiere ver monsieur Duval es a mí ... Entonces, todo cambia. ¿Qué os parece a vosotros? ¿Eh?

MAITÉ (*Un mohín*)

Bueno, tío. Pero no es para que te des tanta importancia ...[47]

RICARDO (*Transición*)

10 ¡Silencio!

TODOS

¡Ay!

RICARDO

¡Y largo de aquí![48] ¡Fuera!

---

[47] *Pero ... importancia* But you needn't put on such airs
[48] *¡ Y largo de aquí!* And get out of here!

MAITÉ

Sí, tío.

MANOLÍN (*Indignado*)

Siempre le echan a uno cuando llega lo mejor. ¡Pues esta vez me voy a quedar escuchando, ea!

TONY

Y que lo digas.[49] ¡Yo también!

(MANOLÍN *y* TONY *salen juntos.* MAITÉ, *por otra puerta.* ROSITA, *por el fondo. Quedan solos* CÁNDIDA *y* RICARDO.) 5

CÁNDIDA

!Ricardo! En este momento me parece que vuelvo a tener otra vez veinte años ...

RICARDO

¿De verdad?

CÁNDIDA

Sí. Tengo la sensación de que ese hombre viene a pedirte mi mano... 10

RICARDO

¡Cándida!

(*Aparece* MARCELO *en el fondo. Tímido y prudente, como siempre, inquiere.*)

MARCELO

"Bon jour, madame ..." ¿Se puede?[50]

CÁNDIDA

¡Marcelo! (MARCELO, *muy dichoso, va hacia* CÁNDIDA *y le besa las manos, que ella le ofrece.*) 15

---

[49] *Y que lo digas* You said it

[50] "*Bon jour, madame ...*" *¿Se puede?* (French) "Good day, madame ..." May I come in?

MARCELO

"Ma chérie!" ¡Su vestido azul! "Je vous vois encore avec cette robe bleue. J'ai l'impression que le temps s'est arrêté ..."[51]

RICARDO (*Desde el sofá. Muy rápido*)

Eso es una tontería ...

MARCELO (*Sorprendido*)

¿Cómo?

CÁNDIDA

5 Pero, ¿no dices que no entiendes el francés?

RICARDO

Es que desde anoche lo estoy recordando mucho.

MARCELO (*Con extrañeza*)

¡Oh! ¿Le sucede algo a su marido?

CÁNDIDA (*Un suspiro*)

Por favor, le ruego que sea usted benévolo con él ... Está muy excitado.

10 (*Desde el fondo, mira piadosamente a su marido y suspira. Luego mira a* MARCELO *y sonríe. Sale. Quedan solos* MARCELO *y* RICARDO. *Un silencio.* RICARDO *está inmóvil en el sofá.* MARCELO, *desde lejos, le contempla y mueve suavemente la cabeza. Después avanza sin ruido, despacito, y se sienta a su lado en el sofá.*)

MARCELO

15 "Monsieur ..." Yo supongo que le extrañará a usted esta visita, pero era necesaria después de lo que anoche ocurrió entre nosotros tres. (*Muy cortés, pero muy firme*) Yo deseo legalizar esta situación ...

[51] "*Ma chérie! ... arrêté*" (French in quotes) My dear! Your blue dress! I am seeing you again in that blue dress. It is as if time had stood still

RICARDO (*Boquiabierto*)

Pero, ¿cree usted que nuestra situación se puede legalizar?

MARCELO (*Muy jovial*)

¡Naturalmente! Todo es cuestión de un poco de buena voluntad por su parte ...

RICARDO

¡Oiga! (*Estupefacto*) ¿Qué es lo que pretende usted de mí?[52]

MARCELO

No se exalte, se lo ruego. Quiero que entre nosotros no haya equívocos ... 5

RICARDO (*Indignado*)

¡Pero si no hay ninguno! ¡Si lo sé todo!

MARCELO

¡Oh, no! Todo, no. (*Sensato*) El marido nunca lo sabe todo ...

RICARDO (*Mirándole. Con un escalofrío*)

¿Qué quiere usted decir?

MARCELO

Verá ... Vengo decidido a hablar claro. Como dice el noble pueblo español: al pan, pan. Y al vino, pan.[53] 10

RICARDO

¡Ca! No es eso ...

MARCELO

¿No?

---

[52] *¿ Qué es ... de mí?* What is it that you expect of me?
[53] *al pan, pan. Y al vino, pan* to call a spade a spade (the Spanish proverb is *al pan, pan y al vino, vino*)

RICARDO

No, señor. (*Con altivez*) ¡Francia no comprenderá jamás al noble pueblo español! (*Transición*) Pues bien: ya que usted lo quiere, hablemos. Pero antes voy a hacerle una pregunta sobre algo que me tiene muy preocupado ...

MARCELO

5 Diga, Diga ...[54]

RICARDO

¡Monsieur Duval! ¿De verdad, de verdad no le soy a usted simpático?

MARCELO

¡Oh! Sí. De verdad ... Lo siento. Lo que me impide sentir simpatía por usted[55] es una cuestión de principios ...

RICARDO (*Asombradísimo*)

10 ¿De qué?

MARCELO

De principios. (*Solemnemente*) ¡Señor mío! Yo soy muy moral ...

RICARDO

¡Ah!

MARCELO (*Con energía*)

¡Sí! Yo soy muy moral. Y usted, en cambio, carece de todo sentido moral. (*Muy enfadado*) ¡Caballero! ¿Qué puedo pensar yo de un
15 hombre que se pasa la vida haciendo el amor a las mujeres casadas?

RICARDO (*Atónito*)

¡Oiga!

---

[54] *Diga, diga* Ask it by all means
[55] *Lo que ... por usted* What prevents me from liking you

MARCELO

¡Silencio! ¿O piensa usted que no conozco toda su vida, paso a paso? Es horrible. Es espantoso. Usted es capaz de todo. Usted no tiene principios, no tiene miramientos, no tiene decoro. Para usted no hay una sola mujer respetable. (*Más indignado todavía*) Cuando usted se ha enamorado[56] de una mujer casada le ha dicho tranquilamente: 5 ¡Te quiero! Y en paz ...

RICARDO (*Mohino*)

Hombre, hombre ...

MARCELO

¡Sí! Se lo ha dicho usted. Y a lo mejor en presencia del pobre marido, porque usted no tiene escrúpulos ...

RICARDO

Hombre, yo ... 10

MARCELO

¡No me interrumpa! (*Con santa razón*) ¿No ha pensado usted nunca que una mujer casada es algo sagrado? ¿No se da usted cuenta de todo lo que hay detrás de ella? Otro hombre. Unos hijos ... ¡Un hogar! ¡Sobre todo, un hogar! ¡Qué escándalo! Pero, señor mío, ¿no le da a usted vergüenza? 15

RICARDO

Hombre ... Le diré.[57]

MARCELO

¡Es usted un monstruo! ¡Un monstruo!

RICARDO (*Con dolorosa decepción*)

¡Vaya un francés! ¡Si parece de los Padres de Familia! ...[58]

---

[56] *Cuando usted se ha enamorado* Whenever you've fallen in love (The perfect tenses here have the value of repeated actions in the past)

[57] *Hombre ... Le diré* Now, look here! (The meaning would vary with the intonation and situation. In this case it seems to be a weak protest)

[58] ¡ *Vaya un francés*! ... *Familia*! What a Frenchman! He might just as well belong to the "Heads of the Family" society ("*Los Padres de Familia*" is a special committee designed for moral censorship, especially in entertainment)

MARCELO

¡Y aún quiere usted que a mí me resulte simpático! Vamos, hombre, vamos ... (*Muy disgustado, se sienta en el sofá en la actitud de un hombre muy cargado de razón.* RICARDO *está ya francamente avergonzado y se acerca a él con mucha humildad.*)

RICARDO

5 Bueno ... ¿No me juzga usted con demasiada severidad? Usted recurre a todas las leyes establecidas por la moral y por la sociedad. Sí, eso es muy cómodo. Pero, ¿no hay otras leyes? ¿Y las leyes del corazón? Cuando un hombre se enamora, ¿debe detenerse a pensar en todo lo que destroza? ¡No! Sería un cobarde. Todo eso, lo que se
10 hunde, ese hogar, esos hijos, ese marido, no importan nada. ¡Nada! Solo importa el triunfo del amor. La verdad del corazón. La única verdad por la que merece la pena vivir ...[59] (*De pronto, se calla en seco. Tiene una brusca transición. Parece que vuelve a escuchar aterrado sus propias palabras. Se vuelve hacia* MARCELO, *y como éste le está mirando,*
15 *hace ya rato,*[60] *sus miradas se cruzan. Un segundo de silencio.*) ¡No! ¡No, no! No es verdad. Todo eso es falso. La única verdad es que la quiero y es mía, ¡sólo mía! porque es mi mujer ... ¡Yo solo tengo derecho a ella! ¿Me oye usted?

MARCELO (*Un silencio. Tímidamente*)

¿La quiere usted?

RICARDO

20 Sí. La quiero con toda mi alma. Creo que nunca la he querido como ahora ...

(*Hunde la cabeza entre las manos.*[61] *Una pausa. Impetuosamente, surgen* MANOLÍN *y* TONY. *Por su actidud y su ímpetu se adivina que han estado escuchando.*)

TONY

25 ¡Profesor! ¡Dígaselo!

---

[59] *La única verdad ... vivir* The only truth which makes life worth living
[60] *como éste ... ya rato* as the latter has been looking at him for some time
[61] *Hunde ... manos* He buries his head in his hands

MANOLÍN

¡Dígaselo ya!

TONY

¡Dígaselo, profesor! ¿No ve usted cómo sufre? ¡Papá! ¡Papá!

MANOLÍN

¡Papá! Escucha ... (*Los dos chicos, corriendo, emocionadísimos, se han sentado uno a cada lado de* RICARDO.)

RICARDO (*Confundido*)

¡Hijos! ¿Qué es esto? 5

MANOLÍN

¡Que todo es mentira, papá!

RICARDO

¿Qué? ... ¿Qué dices?

TONY

¿No comprendes? Todo ha sido una comedia preparada para que tú tengas celos de mamá. Para que vuelvas a quererla ...

MANOLÍN

¡Claro, papá! Como eres tan golfo ... 10

TONY

Todo empezó el último día que no viniste a dormir a casa ... ¿Te acuerdas?

MANOLÍN

¡Hombre! Cómo no se va a acordar, si se fue con Manolita,[62] la mecanógrafa, que estaba imponente ...

---

[62] *Cómo no ... Manolita* How can he help remembering when he went off with Manolita

RICARDO (*Gozosamente confundido*)

Entonces, lo que aquí ha sucedido anoche, ¿no es verdad?

TONY

¡No!

RICARDO

¿Y ese hombre?

TONY

Estaba de acuerdo con mamá.[63]

MANOLÍN

5 Es que el profesor es muy amable ...

RICARDO

¿Eso ha hecho vuestra madre? ¿Ha sido capaz?[64]

TONY

Si, papá. Era su último recurso. Tenías a la pobre mamá tan abandonada ... Te quiere tanto ...

RICARDO

¡Es increíble, fabuloso, fantástico! Y yo he llegado a creer ... He
10 sufrido como si fuera verdad. (*A Marcelo*) De modo que usted y mi mujer han jugado conmigo.

MARCELO

Sí, monsieur.

RICARDO (*Resplandeciente*)

¡Todo es mentira!

---

[63] *Estaba de acuerdo con mamá* He conspired with mother
[64] *¿Ha sido capaz?* She had the courage to do that?

MARCELO

Todo.

RICARDO

¿No está usted enamorado de mi mujer?

MARCELO (*Suavemente*)

¿Quiere usted no hacer más preguntas y correr al lado de su mujer?[65]

RICARDO

Sí, tiene usted razón. No sé en qué estoy pensando. Vamos, hijos. ¡Cándida! ¡Cándida! 5

TONY

¡Mamá!

MANOLÍN

¡Mamá! ¡Mamá!

(*Jubilosamente, salen, por el fondo,* RICARDO, TONY *y* MANOLÍN. MARCELO *queda solo en escena. Se sienta lentamente en el sofá. Entra* CÁNDIDA.) 10

CÁNDIDA

¿Me llaman?

MARCELO

Sí, madame. Es él. La busca, la necesita.

CÁNDIDA

¿Lo sabe?

MARCELO

Sí. Se lo han descubierto los muchachos ...

---

[65] *¿Quiere usted ... su mujer?* Will you please stop asking questions and go quickly to your wife?

CÁNDIDA

¡Oh! Entonces, ha terminado el juego ...

MARCELO

Pero usted ha ganado. Ante la idea de perderla, su marido la quiere como nunca la ha querido. (*Sonríe.*) Ya no iremos a Toledo ...

CÁNDIDA

No, claro ... Ya no es necesario.

MARCELO

5 Tampoco volveremos al Museo del Prado. Ni volveremos a recorrer juntos las callecitas del Madrid antiguo ... Ni volveré a explicarle a usted mi concepto de la socialdemocracia entre los árboles del Retiro.

CÁNDIDA

¡Marcelo! ¿Está usted triste?

MARCELO

10 Un poco ... (*Sonríe.*) Éramos como tres niños jugando. Y, de pronto, yo soy como el niño que ha perdido su juguete. Su querido juguete. (*Un silencio*)

CÁNDIDA

Anoche estuvo usted magnífico.

MARCELO

¿Cree usted?

CÁNDIDA

15 Sí. Cuando dijo usted "Te quiero" había tal acento de verdad en sus palabras ...[66] Casi, casi parecía verdad. Realmente, le hubiera parecido verdad a cualquiera que no hubiera estado en el juego.[67]

---

[66] *había tal acento ... palabras* there was such a ring of truth in your words
[67] *a cualquiera ... juego* to anyone who had not been aware of the game

MARCELO (*Sonríe*)

¡Oh! Usted ... Usted también se portó maravillosamente.

CÁNDIDA

¿No lo hice mal?

MARCELO

No, no. Cuando su marido le dijo: "¿Quién tiene la razón? ¿Él o yo?" usted dijo: "Él, él tiene la razón. Porque dice la verdad. Porque habla con el corazón ..." 5

CÁNDIDA

¿Eso dije? Ya no lo recordaba ...

MARCELO

Es natural. (*Un gran silencio. Avanza unos pasos hacia ella.*) Madame ... Me despido.

CÁNDIDA (*Con sobresalto*)

¿Qué dice usted?

MARCELO

Sí. Mis servicios ya no son necesarios en esta casa. Maité sabe el 10 suficiente francés como para asistir[68] a un teatro de París y comprender la comedia. En cambio, sabe lo suficientemente poco como para no entender[69] las frases de doble sentido ... Me parece que sabe todo el francés que debe saber una señorita española.

CÁNDIDA

¿No le volveremos a ver? 15

MARCELO

No es probable ...

CÁNDIDA

Entonces, adiós, Marcelo ...

---

[68] *como para asistir* to enable her to attend
[69] *como para no entender* to prevent her from understanding

MARCELO

Adiós, madame ... (*Le besa la mano que ella le tiende y marcha hacia el fondo. En la puerta, se detiene.*) ¡Ah! Muchas gracias por su vestido azul ...

CÁNDIDA

No me lo volveré a poner más.

MARCELO

5 Gracias.

(*Sale* MARCELO. *Queda* CÁNDIDA *sola en su sillón y llora suavemente. Entra corriendo* MAITÉ.)

MAITÉ

¡Tía Cándida! ¿Se marcha monsieur Duval? Pero, ¿qué es eso, tía? (*Corre hasta ella, se arrodilla a sus pies y le coge las manos.*) ¿Estás
10 llorando?

CÁNDIDA (*Recogiendo presurosa sus lágrimas*)

Sí ... No. No sé. No sé lo que me ocurre.

MAITÉ (*Asustada*)

¡Tía Candida! ¿No te habrás enamorado de verdad del profesor?[70]

CÁNDIDA

No, no. Claro que no ... Es otra cosa que no podría explicarte. Desde anoche hasta ahora me parece que he sido otra mujer.
15 También era yo la de siempre, ¿sabes? Yo estaba en la broma y sabía que todo era un juego. Pero, al mismo tiempo, era una pobre mujer que vivía por primera vez una gran aventura ... Óyeme, pequeña. Cuando seas mayor, cuando seas de verdad una mujer, no juegues ... No se puede jugar. No se sabe quién juega con quién.
20 Es tan peligroso poner como prenda el corazón ...[71] Lo mejor es vivir tomando lo que nos dé la vida. Risas o lágrimas. Pero sin jugar. ¿Comprendes, Maité, comprendes?

---

[70] *¿No te habrás ... profesor?* I wonder if you actually fell in love with the professor?

[71] *Es tan peligroso ... el corazón* It's so dangerous to use the heart as a forfeit

MAITÉ

¡Tía Cándida!

(*Entra* RICARDO, *seguido de* TONY. *Va hacia* CÁNDIDA. MAITÉ *y* TONY, *juntos, se retiran a un lado.*)

RICARDO

¡Cándida!

CÁNDIDA

¡Ricardo! 5

RICARDO

Calla, calla. Ni una palabra. No digas nada. Todo me lo merezco. Pero, desde hoy, te aseguro que todo cambiará. Ahora sí que soy otro. Buen juego te has traído.[72] Buena lección. Oye ... Me gustaria que me contaras. ¿Cómo empezó esto? ¿Cómo se te ocurrió esta idea? 10

CÁNDIDA

Pero si no se me ocurrió a mí ...

RICARDO

¿No?

MAITÉ

No, no, tío Ricardo. Se me ocurrió a mí.[73]

RICARDO (*Atónito*)

¿A ti?

TONY (*Muy contento*)

Sí, papá. Todo es cosa de Maité,[74] que sabe mucho ... 15

---

[72] *Buen juego te has traído* You certainly played quite a game
[73] *Se me ocurrió a mí* It was *my* idea
[74] *Todo es cosa de Maité* The whole thing is Maité's doing

RICARDO

¡Ah! ¿Sí?

MAITÉ (*Orgullosísima. Se ríe muy divertida*)

Pero todavía no sabe lo mejor. La que llamó anoche al Círculo era yo.

RICARDO (*Mirándola fijamente*)

¿Tú? ...

CÁNDIDA

5 Sí, sí. ¡Ella!

TONY

¡Ella! ¡Ella!

MAITÉ

¡Yo! ¿Qué te parece? (RICARDO *se queda mirando fijamente a su sobrina durante un segundo y casi pega un grito.*)

RICARDO

¡Maité!

TODOS (*Asustados*)

10 ¡Ay!

RICARDO

De manera que este infierno en el que he vivido desde anoche, te lo debo a ti ...

MAITÉ (*Muy asustada*)

¡Ay, tío Ricardo! No me mires así ...

RICARDO

¡Maité! Prepara tus maletas. Se acabaron los estudios en Madrid.[75]
15 Esta noche coges el tren, y mañana vas a hacer de las tuyas[76] en provincias, con tu madre ... ¡Vivo!

Se acabaron ... Madrid You're through studying in Madrid
vas a hacer de las tuyas you go play your tricks

MAITÉ

Pero tío Ricardo ... (*Llorando*) ¿Es que me echas?

RICARDO (*Furioso*)

¡Sí!

CÁNDIDA

¡Ricardo!

TONY

¡Papá!

MAITÉ

Tío, por Dios. Yo no quiero irme de esta casa. No me eches. No me eches. Yo no puedo vivir sin vosotros. Yo no quiero, no quiero ... (Y, *desconsolada, ahoga sus sollozos abrazándose con verdadero ímpetu a* TONY.) 5

TONY

¡Maité!

MAITÉ

Yo te quiero muchísimo, tío Ricardo. Yo quiero mucho a tía Cándida ... (*Se abraza otra vez al muchacho.*) 10

TONY (*Muy apurado*)

Pero, chica ... ¡Que me ahogas![77]

RICARDO (*Asombradísimo*)

Oye. ¿Qué te parece? Dice que no puede vivir sin ti y sin mí y mira ...

CÁNDIDA

Ya, ya ... Es curioso. (*Contempla a los muchachos y sonríe. En voz baja*) ¡Ricardo! Creo que cuando son primos hermanos hay que pedir permiso al Papa ... 15

---

[77] ¡ *Que me ahogas*! You're choking me!

RICARDO

¿Tú crees? Pero, ¿será posible?

CÁNDIDA

Ya ves. (RICARDO *avanza hacia los chicos y separa, cariñosamente, a* MAITÉ *y a* TONY.)

RICARDO

¡Oh! Está bien, mujer, está bien. No te irás. Pero suéltalo ...

MAITÉ

5 ¡Tío de mi alma![78] (MAITÉ *abraza y besa a* RICARDO. *Luego corre hacia* CÁNDIDA *y se refugia en sus brazos.*) ¡Tía Cándida!

CÁNDIDA

¡Chiquilla!

RICARDO

Oye, hijo ... ¿Qué las das?[79]

TONY

¿Yo? Pero si no hago nada, papá. ¡Si es que se declaran ellas![80]

RICARDO

10 ¡Caray! ¿Eso es verdad? (*Muy interesado*) Cuéntame, hombre, cuéntame ...

(*En ese momento entra* ROSITA, *cruza la escena muy indignada, de izquierda a derecha. Casi va llorando de coraje.*)

---

[78] *¡Tío de mi alma!* My darling uncle!

[79] *¿Qué las das?* How do you do it? (*i.e.*, What do you give the girls to attract them like this?)

[80] *¡Si es que se declaran ellas!* But *they* are the ones who propose!

ROSITA

¡Señora! Tengo que advertir a la señora que si la señora no riñe al señorito Manolín yo no puedo continuar en la casa. Porque, para que usted lo sepa ...[81] (*Indignadísima*) ¡El señorito Manolín es un granuja!

(*Sale. Todos se miran asombrados. En la puerta aparece* MANOLÍN, *tan tranquilo, que atraviese la escena con las manos en los bolsillos del pantalón. Porque ya es un hombre.*) 5

TODOS (*Mirándole*)

¡Manolín!

MANOLÍN

¿Qué pasa? ¿Por qué me miráis así? ¡Ah, vamos! Eso es que Rosita os ha venido con el cuento ...[82] 10

RICARDO

¡Niño!

MANOLÍN

Pero si no ha sido nada ... Total, que hemos tropezado en el pasillo y dice que yo la he dado un beso. Pero yo no me he dado cuenta ... Palabra. Habrá sido sin querer. ¡Hay que ver! Cómo se pone esta chica por nada ...[83] (*Y sale silbando con todo desparpajo. Todos le siguen con la mirada, verdaderamente atónitos.*) 15

RICARDO

Oye, Cándida. ¡Este chico es un fresco!

CÁNDIDA

Sí, Ricardo. Este ... ¡Este es igual que tú!

TELÓN

[81] *para que usted lo sepa* I want you to know
[82] *Eso es que ... cuento* It's because Rosita has come to tattle on me
[83] *Habrá sido ... por nada* I probably did it unintentionally. Now, really! This girl makes such a fuss over nothing

Oral Pattern Drills

General Directions and Examples of Pattern Drills

For the Instructor: Some Basic Principles in the Use of Pattern Drills

This section is designed to offer maximum opportunity for supervised class drill leading to increased oral mastery, and to provide maximum flexibility in drill methods and techniques. Although some of the material may be easily adapted to language laboratory techniques, the success of these drills is contingent on effective teaching, and not on the use of mechanical aids or devices.

The basic assumption here, in keeping with both modern and traditional concepts of learning, is that, while the end result of a language drill should be to produce an automatic response, the drill itself must be a conscious, deliberate effort based on an understanding of the principle involved. This principle in turn would be reached by inductive methods. Conscious, and not mechanical repetition is especially vital at this level of learning.

The author recommends the following basic principles for drilling:

1) *Understanding the construction:* The student must understand the construction of the pattern drill model *before* he drills.

2) *Memorization of the pattern and emphasis on one variable:* In order to concentrate on the single variable being drilled, the student should memorize the pattern and the verb phrases in the Verb Index Table.

3) *Conscious—not automatic—drill:* All drill must be conscious and deliberate regardless of the speed achieved. Supervised drill for

new material is essential to control the learning process in these drills.

4) *Spaced learning:* Frequent repetition of a specific drill over a long period of time will prove more effective than concentrated drill.

The Verb Index Table provides only the basic forms for drilling typical structural patterns in the Pattern Drill section, although it may also be used for many other types of constructions. For visual efficiency and drill purposes, only the first and third persons in the singular appear. Pattern Drills based on the Index are limited to these persons but other forms may be introduced at the discretion of the instructor.

Related tenses (i.e., Indicative and Subjunctive, Preterite and Imperfect, Future and Conditional) are in adjoining columns for drill purposes. The simplest possible explanations for verb irregularities are given in the section called Short-Cuts for Verb Irregularities, which follows the Verb Index Table.

The Pattern Drills and Exercises are composed of some high frequency constructions taken from the text with a few necessary changes for the sake of effective drilling. The first five drills are based on the Verb Index Table and are necessarily limited to flexible constructions which may be used with different verbs. Except for the first few pattern drill models, the assignment of specific verbs from the Index is left to the instructor.

Because of its difficulty and importance in oral and written expression, the Subjunctive constructions have been given major emphasis in the Drills. However, other important constructions such as the Imperfect and Preterite, or *ser* and *estar*, are covered in the Drills or in the Exercises that follow. The emphasis is always on the construction and not on the verb form *per se*. Since the patterns *within* the Drills and Exercises are fairly sequential in the text, the instructor may assign one or two patterns from each exercise simultaneously. This provides opportunity for repetition and spaced learning.

For the Student: Drill Procedures and Examples of Oral Drills

How to Use the Verb Index Table in Pattern Drills

1. Read the Directions preceding each major drill and understand exactly what is required in that particular drill construction.

2. Study and memorize the first pattern model before starting to drill.

3. Find the verbs assigned for that pattern in the Verb Index Table.

4. For each new verb, choose the verb phase (in the end column) that makes sense with the pattern and memorize each phrase as you drill.

5. In drilling, you merely substitute the *underlined phrase* or *phrases* of the pattern (the variable) with the corresponding form of the verbs.

6. Check and repeat the pattern with each new verb phrase several times without looking, but concentrate always on the variable.

7. Review frequently and by groups, using the Infinitive as a guide.

8. Before working on Pattern Drills, study the illustrations on oral drills so that the procedure is perfectly clear.

9. Keep in mind these basic principles for oral pattern drills:
   (*a*) Understand the construction *before* you begin to drill.
   (*b*) Memorize the construction *before* you drill.
   (*c*) Concentrate on the variable (the underlined phrase) while you drill.
   (*d*) Review frequently at spaced intervals.

EXAMPLES OF ORAL PATTERN DRILLS

From Drill One (Single Pattern): The Present Subjunctive

Directions: Substitute the *underlined phrases* with assigned verb phrases from the Verb Index Table using the same constructions as those in the pattern models.

1. *Pattern given:* Espero que él <u>esté aquí</u>
   Drill assignment: Radical Changing Verbs 1 through 10 in Verb Index
   Oral Drill: Find the verbs in the Verb Index Table and drill as follows:
   (pensar) Espero que él <u>lo piense bien</u>

(perder) Espero que no pierda nada
(contar) Espero que (no) le cuente mi vida

(Continue drilling as above with other Radical Changing Verbs)

2. *Pattern given:* Es posible que no vaya a casa
Drill assignment: Assigned verbs from the Verb Index Table
Oral Drill: The same as above, substituting verb phrases for *no vaya*

From Drill Three (Double Pattern): Contrasting the Indicative and Subjunctive

Directions: Contrast the function of the Indicative and Subjunctive moods in the following double patterns by substituting the *underlined phrases* with those assigned from the Verb Index Table.

Patterns given: (Indic.) Creo que él se va de aquí (Subj.) No creo que él se vaya de aquí
Drill assignment: Assigned verbs from the Index such as *buscar*, *llegar*, etc.
(buscar) Creo que él lo busca ... No creo que él lo busque
(llegar) Creo que él llega a tiempo ... No creo que él llegue a tiempo

(Continue the drill with the assigned verbs as above)

	Infinitive	Familiar Imperative	Present Participle	Past Participle	Present	Present Subjunc
I.	**Regular Verbs:**					
1.	hablar	habla (tú) hablad (vosotros)	hablando	hablado	hablo (yo) habla (él)	hable (y hable (é
2.	comer	come comed	comiendo	comido	como come	coma coma
3.	vivir	vive vivid	viviendo	vivido	vivo vive	viva viva
II.	**Irregular Verbs:**					
1.	andar*	anda andad	andando	andado	ando anda	ande ande
2.	caber*	cabe cabed	cabiendo	cabido	quepo cabe	quepa quepa
3.	caer	cae caed	cayendo	caído	caigo cae	caiga caiga
4.	dar	da dad	dando	dado	doy da	dé dé
5.	decir*	di decid	diciendo	dicho	digo dice	diga diga
6.	estar*	está estad	estando	estado	estoy está	esté esté
7.	haber*		habiendo	habido	he ha (hay)	haya haya
8.	hacer*	haz haced	haciendo	hecho	hago hace	haga haga
9.	ir	ve id	yendo	ido	voy va	vaya vaya
10.	oir	oye oíd	oyendo	oído	oigo oye	oiga oiga
11.	poder*		pudiendo	podido	puedo puede	pueda pueda

* Preterite endings like "estar" (see "Short-Cuts for Verb Irregularities")

FOR PATTERN DRILLS

Preterite	Imperfect	Imperfect Subjunctive	Future	Conditional	Verb Phrases for Drills
hablé	hablaba	hablara	hablaré	hablaría	hablar mucho
habló	hablaba	hablara	hablará	hablaría	hablarle
comí	comía	comiera	comeré	comería	comer bien
comió	comía	comiera	comerá	comería	comer en casa
viví	vivía	viviera	viviré	viviría	vivir bien
vivió	vivía	viviera	vivirá	viviría	vivir en Madrid
anduve	andaba	anduviera	andaré	andaría	andar por aquí
anduvo	andaba	anduviera	andará	andaría	andar solo
cupe	cabía	cupiera	cabré	cabría	caber bien aquí
cupo	cabía	cupiera	cabrá	cabría	caber en mi sitio
caí	caía	cayera	caeré	caería	caer en el suelo
cayó	caía	cayera	caerá	caería	caer(le) bien
di	daba	diera	daré	daría	dar(le) el libro
dio	daba	diera	dará	daría	dárselo
dije	decía	dijera	diré	diría	decírselo
dijo	decía	dijera	dirá	diría	decir la verdad
estuve	estaba	estuviera	estaré	estaría	estar en casa
estuvo	estaba	estuviera	estará	estaría	estar enfermo
hube	había	hubiera	habré	habría	haber gente
hubo	había	hubiera	habrá	habría	haber llegado
hice	hacía	hiciera	haré	haría	hacer algo
hizo	hacía	hiciera	hará	haría	no hacer nada
fui	iba	fuera	iré	iría	ir a casa
fue	iba	fuera	irá	iría	ir a verla
oí	oía	oyera	oiré	oiría	oir a alguien
oyó	oía	oyera	oirá	oiría	no oir nada
pude	podía	pudiera	podré	podría	poder dárselo
pudo	podía	pudiera	podrá	podría	poder venir

	Infinitive	Familiar Imperative	Present Participle	Past Participle	Present	Present Subjunctive
12.	poner*	pon poned	poniendo	puesto	pongo pone	ponga ponga
13.	querer*	quiere quered	queriendo	querido	quiero quiere	quiera quiera
14.	saber*	sabe sabed	sabiendo	sabido	sé sabe	sepa sepa
15.	salir	sal salid	saliendo	salido	salgo sale	salga salga
16.	ser	sé sed	siendo	sido	soy es	sea sea
17.	tener*	ten tened	teniendo	tenido	tengo tiene	tenga tenga
18.	traer*	trae traed	trayendo	traído	traigo trae	traiga traiga
19.	valer	val valed	valiendo	valido	valgo vale	valga valga
20.	venir*	ven venid	viniendo	venido	vengo viene	venga venga
21.	ver	ve ved	viendo	visto	veo ve	vea vea

III. Radical Changing Verbs:

	Infinitive	Familiar Imperative	Present Participle	Past Participle	Present	Present Subjunctive
1.	contar (ue)	cuenta contad	contando	contado	cuento cuenta	cuente cuente
2.	dormir (ue, u)	duerme dormid	durmiendo	dormido	duermo duerme	duerma duerma
3.	jugar (ue)	juega jugad	jugando	jugado	juego juega	juegue juegue
4.	pedir (i, i)	pide pedid	pidiendo	pedido	pido pide	pida pida
5.	pensar (ie)	piensa pensad	pensando	pensado	pienso piensa	piense piense
6.	perder (ie)	pierde perded	perdiendo	perdido	pierdo pierde	pierda pierda

for Pattern Drills

Preterite	Imperfect	Imperfect Subjunctive	Future	Conditional	Verb Phrases for Drills
puse	ponía	pusiera	pondré	pondría	poner la mesa
puso	ponía	pusiera	pondrá	pondría	ponerlo aquí
quise	quería	quisiera	querré	querría	querer verlo
quiso	quería	quisiera	querrá	querría	querer dárselo
supe	sabía	supiera	sabré	sabría	saber mucho
supo	sabía	supiera	sabrá	sabría	saberlo todo
salí	salía	saliera	saldré	saldría	salir de casa
salió	salía	saliera	saldrá	saldría	salir al cine
fui	era	fuera	seré	sería	ser famoso
fue	era	fuera	será	sería	ser un caballero (una señora)
tuve	tenía	tuviera	tendré	tendría	tener algo
tuvo	tenía	tuviera	tendrá	tendría	no tener nada
traje	traía	trajera	traeré	traería	traer sombrero
trajo	traía	trajera	traerá	traería	traerlo puesto
valí	valía	valiera	valdré	valdría	valer mucho
valió	valía	valiera	valdrá	valdría	no valer nada
vine	venía	viniera	vendré	vendría	venir en seguida
vino	venía	viniera	vendrá	vendría	venir a enseñar
vi	veía	viera	veré	vería	ver a alguien
vio	veía	viera	verá	vería	no ver a nadie
conté	contaba	contara	contaré	contaría	contarle mi vida
contó	contaba	contara	contará	contaría	contársela
dormí	dormía	durmiera	dormiré	dormiría	dormir mucho
durmió	dormía	durmiera	dormirá	dormiría	dormirse allí
jugué	jugaba	jugara	jugaré	jugaría	jugar con eso
jugó	jugaba	jugara	jugará	jugaría	jugar sin pensar
pedí	pedía	pidiera	pediré	pediría	pedir(le) dinero
pidió	pedía	pidiera	pedirá	pediría	pedírselo
pensé	pensaba	pensara	pensaré	pensaría	pensar en algo
pensó	pensaba	pensara	pensará	pensaría	pensarlo bien
perdí	perdía	perdiera	perderé	perdería	perder algo
perdió	perdía	perdiera	perderá	perdería	no perder nada

	Infinitive	Familiar Imperative	Present Participle	Past Participle	Present	Present Subjunctive
7.	reir (i, i)	ríe reíd	riendo	reído	río ríe	ría ría
8.	repetir (i, i)	repite repetid	repitiendo	repetido	repito repite	repita repita
9.	sentir (ie, i)	siente sentid	sintiendo	sentido	siento siente	sienta sienta
10.	volver (ue)	vuelve volved	volviendo	vuelto	vuelvo vuelve	vuelva vuelva

IV. Orthographic Changing Verbs:

	Infinitive	Familiar Imperative	Present Participle	Past Participle	Present	Present Subjunctive
1.	averiguar (gu-gü)	averigua averiguad	averiguando	averiguado	averiguo averigua	averigüe averigüe
2.	buscar (c-qu)	busca buscad	buscando	buscado	busco busca	busque busque
3.	coger (g-j)	coge coged	cogiendo	cogido	cojo coge	coja coja
4.	conocer (c-zc)	conoce conoced	conociendo	conocido	conozco conoce	conozca conozca
5.	convencer (c-z)	convence convenced	convenciendo	convencido	convenzo convence	convenza convenza
6.	dirigir (g-j)	dirige dirigid	dirigiendo	dirigido	dirijo dirige	dirija dirija
7.	distinguir (gu-g)	distingue distinguid	distinguiendo	distinguido	distingo distingue	distinga distinga
8.	lanzar (z-c)	lanza lanzad	lanzando	lanzado	lanzo lanza	lance lance
9.	llegar (g-gu)	llega llegad	llegando	llegado	llego llega	llegue llegue
10.	producir* (c-zc)	produce producid	produciendo	producido	produzco produce	produzca produzca

V. Both Radical and Orthographic Changing Verbs:

	Infinitive	Familiar Imperative	Present Participle	Past Participle	Present	Present Subjunctive
1.	empezar (ie) (z-c)	empieza empezad	empezando	empezado	empiezo empieza	empiece empiece

)R PATTERN DRILLS

eterite	Imperfect	Imperfect Subjunctive	Future	Condi- tional	Verb Phrases for Drills
	reía	riera	reiré	reiría	reirse mucho
	reía	riera	reirá	reiría	reirse de alguien
etí	repetía	repitiera	repetiré	repetiría	repetir la frase
itió	repetía	repitiera	repetirá	repetiría	repetirla
tí	sentía	sintiera	sentiré	sentiría	sentirse mal
tió	sentía	sintiera	sentirá	sentiría	sentirlo mucho
lví	volvía	volviera	volveré	volvería	volver a casa
vió	volvía	volviera	volverá	volvería	volver a hacerlo
erigüé	averiguaba	averiguara	averiguaré	averiguaría	averiguar eso
eriguó	averiguaba	averiguara	averiguará	averiguaría	averiguarlo
squé	buscaba	buscara	buscaré	buscaría	buscar algo
scó	buscaba	buscara	buscará	buscaría	buscarlo
gí	cogía	cogiera	cogeré	cogería	coger el libro
gió	cogía	cogiera	cogerá	cogería	cogerlo
ocí	conocía	conociera	conoceré	conocería	conocerlo
oció	conocía	conociera	conocerá	conocería	conocerlas
vencí	convencía	convenciera	convenceré	convencería	convencerla
venció	convencía	convenciera	convencerá	convencería	convencerse de ello
igí	dirigía	dirigiera	dirigiré	dirigiría	dirigirse a casa
igió	dirigía	dirigiera	dirigirá	dirigiría	dirigirse a ella
tinguí	distinguía	distinguiera	distinguiré	distinguiría	distinguir algo
tinguió	distinguía	distinguiera	distinguirá	distinguiría	distinguirlo
cé	lanzaba	lanzara	lanzaré	lanzaría	lanzar un grito
zó	lanzaba	lanzara	lanzará	lanzaría	lanzarlo
gué	llegaba	llegara	llegaré	llegaría	llegar a casa
gó	llegaba	llegara	llegará	llegaría	llegar a tiempo
oduje	producía	produjera	produciré	produciría	no producir nada
odujo	producía	produjera	producirá	produciría	no producirlo
pecé	empezaba	empezara	empezaré	empezaría	empezar a leer
pezó	empezaba	empezara	empezará	empezaría	empezarlo

	Infinitive	Familiar Imperative	Present Participle	Past Participle	Present	Present Subjunct
2.	negar (ie) (g-gu)	niega negad	negando	negado	niego niega	niegue niegue
3.	seguir (i) (gu-g)	sigue seguid	siguiendo	seguido	sigo sigue	siga siga

VI. Verbs with Stems Ending in a Vowel:

1.	enviar	envía enviad	enviando	enviado	envío envía	envíe envíe
2.	huir	huye huíd	huyendo	huído	huyo huye	huya huya
3.	leer	lee leed	leyendo	leído	leo lee	lea lea

Preterite	Imperfect	Imperfect Subjunctive	Future	Conditional	Verb Phrases for Drills
negué	negaba	negara	negaré	negaría	negarlo
negó	negaba	negara	negará	negaría	negarse a ir
seguí	seguía	siguiera	seguiré	seguiría	seguir el camino
siguió	seguía	siguiera	seguirá	seguiría	seguir hablando
envié	enviaba	enviara	enviaré	enviaría	enviarle una carta
envió	enviaba	enviara	enviará	enviaría	enviársela
huí	huía	huyera	huiré	huiría	huir de casa
huyó	huía	huyera	huirá	huiría	huir llorando
leí	leía	leyera	leeré	leería	leer la carta
leyó	leía	leyera	leerá	leería	leérsela a ella

Short-Cuts for Verb Irregularities

Regular Verbs

All regular verbs are conjugated like *hablar*, *comer*, and *vivir*.

Irregular Verbs

Verbs marked with an asterisk (*) have the same endings in the Preterite as *estar: estuve*, *estuviste*, *estuvo*, *estuvimos*, *estuvisteis*, *estuvieron*. The Preterite third plural of *decir* and *traer* are *dijeron* and *trajeron* without the *i*. Note the similarity between many forms in the Present Indicative (first singular) and the Present Subjunctive, the Preterite (third plural) and the Imperfect Subjunctive, and the Future and Conditional stems. The Present of *haber* for the Present Perfect tense is: *he*, *has*, *ha*, *hemos*, *habéis*, *han*. Note similarities with future endings.

Radical Changing Verbs

In radical changing (R.C.) verbs, the radical vowels *e* or *o* (*jugar* is an exception) change to a diphthong or to another vowel under certain conditions. The radical vowel is always the last vowel of the stem (*repet–ir*). There are two general principles governing these changes, depending on whether the radical vowel is stressed or unstressed:

1) The *stressed* radical vowel: In all R.C. verbs (*–ar*, *–er*, or *–ir*) the stressed *o* changes to *ue* and the stressed *e* changes to *ie*, except in certain *–ir* verbs like *pedir* in which the stressed *e* changes only to an *i*. This change occurs in the Present Indicative and Present Subjunctive in the first, second, third singular, and third plural and in the *tú* form only of the familiar Imperative.

2) The *unstressed* radical vowel: In *–ir* verbs only, the unstressed *o* changes to *u* and the unstressed *e* changes to *i* when immediately followed by stressed (not necessarily "accented") *a*, *ió*, or *ie*. This change occurs in the Present Participle, the Present Subjunctive in the first and second plural, the Preterite third persons singular and plural, and all of the Imperfect Subjunctive. Note that in *reir* (no accent) *ri–ió* becomes simply *rio* (no accent), and *ri–ieron* becomes *rieron*.

Orthographic Changing Verbs

These verbs change the consonant at the end of the verb stem (*busc–ar*) in order to preserve the original sound of the infinitive (*buscar: busque*). The consonant changes are indicated in the Verb Index Table immediately after the infinitive. All orthographic changing verbs will change in all forms of the Present Subjunctive, but note that *–ar* verbs change in the Preterite (first singular only), while the *–er* and *–ir* verbs change in the Present (first singular only). Verbs listed in the vocabulary with similar stem endings change like those in the Verb Index Table.

Verbs with Stems Ending in a Vowel

In *–uir* verbs, insert *y* before *o*, *a*, or *e* (*huyo*, *huya*, *huye*) and change *io* or *ie* to *yo* and *ye* (*huyó*, *huyeron*).

Verbs ending in *–eer* change unstressed *i* to *y* before vowels (*le–iendo* becomes *leyendo*).

Verbs ending in *–iar* or *–uar* require a written accent on the *i* or *u* if the endings are not stressed (*envío*, *continúo*, but *continuamos*).

PATTERN DRILLS* AND EXERCISES BASED ON JUEGO DE NIÑOS

Drill One: The Infinitive and Present Subjunctive

Directions: Drill by substituting the *underlined phrases* in each pattern drill model with the assigned verbs from the Verb Index Table. Learn the verb phrases (last column) with the Infinitive pattern drill below, then use them in the other patterns with appropriate constructions. In drilling with the verb phrases make the changes for agreement if needed (i.e., *mi* instead of *su*) and use a negative if it makes more sense. Understand and memorize each model before drilling with other verbs.

INFINITIVE VERB PHRASES:

1. *Pattern:* Es necesario darle una buena lección.
   Drill: With the first phrase of all Infinitive Verb Phrases (except *haber*) in the Verb Index Table, last column
   Oral Drill: Es necesario (no) hablar mucho,
   Es necesario comer bien, etc.
2. *Pattern:* Me gustaría volver a empezar
   Drill: With the second phrase of all Infinitive Verb Phrases

PRESENT SUBJUNCTIVE:

1. *Pattern:* Es mejor que (yo) me quite los zapatos
   Drill: Irregular Verbs 1 through 11 in Index
   Oral Drill: Es mejor que (yo) ande por aquí,
   Es mejor que (yo) quepa en mi sitio, etc.
2. *Pattern:* Es necesario que (él) me lo explique todo
   Drill: Irregular Verbs 12 through 21 in Index
3. *Pattern:* No quiere que (yo) la compadezca
   Drill: Radical Changing Verbs 1 through 10
4. *Pattern:* Le he dicho a usted que se calle
   Drill: Orthographic Changing Verbs 1 through 10
5. *Pattern:* No perdona que el otro sea mas feo que él
   Drill: Radical and Orthographic Changing Verbs 1 through 3, and Verbs with Stems Ending in a Vowel 1 through 3
6. *Pattern:* ¿Será posible que (ella) no sepa hacerlo?
   Drill: (With this and following patterns, verbs assigned in class from the Verb Index Table)

* Drills One through Five are with the Verb Index Table, pp. 120–127

7. *Pattern:* A veces dudo que sea usted francés
8. *Pattern:* Ella siente mucho que (yo) ignore estas cosas
9. *Pattern:* Le ruego a usted que sea bueno con él
10. *Pattern:* Ella ha ordenado que (yo) ponga flores en su cuarto
11. *Pattern:* No sé qué pensará su madre cuando termine sus estudios
12. *Pattern:* Hemos hecho esto para que él vuelva a enamorarse de ella
13. *Pattern:* No conozco a nadie que (no) le tenga lástima
14. *Pattern:* No creo que (ella) haya aprendido mucho francés
15. *Pattern:* (El) espera que (yo) me haya puesto el vestido azul

Drill Two: The Imperfect Subjunctive

Directions: Substitute the *underlined phrases* with other assigned verbs, using the same constructions as in the patterns given below.

1. *Pattern:* Lo mejor sería que él los viera juntos
   Drill: Assigned verbs from the Index such as *decir*, *estar*, etc.
   Oral Drill: Lo mejor sería que se lo dijera, etc.
2. *Pattern:* No podría soportar que él tuviera lástima de mí
3. *Pattern:* Me gustaría que él también sufriera
4. *Pattern:* Nunca creyó que yo fuera tan egoísta
5. *Pattern:* Me alegraría de que usted volviera a enamorarse de ella
6. *Pattern:* Ella esperaba que fuera verdad
7. *Pattern:* El no creía que yo hubiera estado en Toledo
8. *Pattern:* Era imposible que él lo hubiera sabido
9. *Pattern:* Buscaba una mujer que fuera sencilla
10. *Pattern:* Habla como si estuviera en su casa
11. *Pattern:* Ha sufrido como si hubiera sido verdad
12. *Pattern:* Si yo tuviera miedo no estaría aquí
13. *Pattern:* Estaría furioso si se enterara
14. *Pattern:* Lo hicieron para que él volviera con ella
15. *Pattern:* No querían irse hasta que el profesor llegara

Drill Three: Contrasting the Indicative and Subjunctive

Directions: Contrast the function of the Indicative and Subjunctive moods in the following double patterns by substituting the *underlined phrases* with those assigned from the Verb Index Table. Drill *across* for each verb with both tenses. Understand the reason for the contrast and memorize the double pattern before drilling.

1. *Patterns:* Espero verlo   Espero que Vd. lo vea
   Drill: Assigned verbs from Index, such as *salir*, *saber*, *ser*, etc.
   Oral Drill: Espero salir de casa   Espero que usted salga de casa
   Espero saberlo todo   Espero que Vd. lo sepa todo, etc.
2. *Patterns:* Creo que se puede legalizar   No creo que se pueda legalizar
3. *Patterns:* Será mejor acostarse   Será mejor que (yo) me acueste
4. *Patterns:* No es necesario ser guapo   No es necesario que él sea guapo
5. *Patterns:* Se alegra de estar aquí   Se alegra de que yo esté aquí
6. *Patterns:* (Yo) quisiera salir sola   (Yo) quisiera que ella saliera sola
7. *Patterns:* Dígale que tiene que irse   Dígale que se vaya
8. *Patterns:* ¿ Quieres irte con ellos?   ¿ Quieres que yo me vaya con ellos?
9. *Patterns:* Le dije (a ella) que (yo) no la vería más   Le dije (a ella) que no me viera más
10. *Patterns:* No quería hablar de esto   No quería que Vd. hablara de esto
11. *Patterns:* Cuando se enamora, siempre pierde el apetito   Cuando se enamore, perderá el apetito
12. *Patterns:* Aunque él me lo dijo, no se lo creí   Aunque él me lo dijera, no se lo creería
13. *Patterns:* Hay alguien aquí que la conoce   No hay nadie aquí que la conozca
14. *Patterns:* Si yo voy, ella no irá   Si yo fuera, ella no iría
15. *Patterns:* Si Vd. vuelve, ella se pondrá furiosa   Si Vd. volviera, ella se pondría furiosa
16. *Patterns:* Si se va al Círculo vuelve tarde   Si se fuera al Círculo volvería tarde
17. *Patterns:* Si se ha ido al Círculo volverá tarde   Si se hubiera ido al Círculo volvería tarde
18. *Patterns:* Si se fue al Círculo volvió tarde   Si se hubiera ido al Círculo habría vuelto tarde

Drill Four: The Imperfect and Preterite

Directions: Substitute the *underlined Preterite* or *Imperfect phrases* with other assigned verbs from the Verb Index Table. Keep the same tense relationship as that given in the pattern.

REPEATED OR SIMULTANEOUS ACTIONS:

1. *Pattern:* Cuando la veía le hablaba de mi familia

   Drill: Assigned verbs from the Index, such as *pedir*, *leer*, *ir*, etc.

   Oral Drill: Cuando la veía me pedía dinero

   Cuando la veía me leía la carta, etc.

2. *Pattern:* Siempre que miraba el reloj eran las dos de la tarde
3. *Pattern:* El sabía que todo era un juego
4. *Pattern:* Era una pobre mujer que vivía por primera vez
5. *Pattern:* ¿ Creía usted que era la primera vez?

CONSECUTIVE, COMPLETED, OR LIMITED ACTIONS:

1. *Pattern:* Ayer me encontré a una amiga y se me declaró
2. *Pattern:* La llevó a cenar a una taberna y le contó su vida
3. *Pattern:* Cuando se hizo de día la llevé a desayunar
4. *Pattern:* Cuando llegamos al Círculo (yo) paré el coche
5. *Pattern:* El verano pasado me escapé y estuve fuera tres días

COMBINED DESCRIPTIVE AND COMPLETED ACTIONS:

1. *Pattern:* Estaba allí cuando él me trajo un recado
2. *Pattern:* Tú te empeñaste en que era una broma
3. *Pattern:* Usted llevaba un vestido azul cuando yo la conocí
4. *Pattern:* Como estábamos tan ocupados no tuve tiempo de dártelo
5. *Pattern:* A la vuelta nos dijo que venía de Pamplona

Drill Five: *Hacer* with Expressions of Time

Directions: Substitute the *underlined phrases* with other assigned verbs from the Verb Index Table, using the same constructions as in the patterns given.

HACER MEANING "FOR":

1. *Pattern:* Hace una hora que estoy aquí

   Drill: Assigned verbs from the Index such as *andar*, *decir*, etc.

   Oral Drill: Hace una hora que ando por aquí

   Hace una hora que se lo digo, etc.

2. *Pattern:* Desde hace quince días mi vida está en peligro
3. *Pattern:* Hace un año que estoy enamorado de usted
4. *Pattern:* Hacía un año que vivía en Madrid

5. *Pattern:* Hacía tiempo que no llegaba tan tarde
6. *Pattern:* Hacía varios meses que estudiaba francés

HACER MEANING "AGO":
1. *Pattern:* Hace una hora que estuvo aquí
   Drill: Assigned verbs from the Index such as *ir*, *salir*, etc.
   Oral Drill: Hace una hora que fue a verla
   Hace una hora que salió al cine, etc.
2. *Pattern:* La conocí hace dos años
3. *Pattern:* Hace un rato la dejó en su casa
4. *Pattern:* Hace varios años las conocía muy bien
5. *Pattern:* Hace algunos meses él estaba en París
6. *Pattern:* Estaba estudiando allí hace menos de una hora

Exercise One: Sequence of Tense Changes in Both Indicative and Subjunctive

Directions: The following sentences are taken directly from the text, *Juego de niños*, with occasional minor changes, and divided according to acts. The Verb Index is not involved since only the tenses are changed. Analyze and memorize the given sentence. Then complete the second version by changing the *underlined tenses* so as to conform in sequence with the change in the first verb tense. Each sentence presents different problems in sequence. Study the example before making the changes.

EXAMPLE:
Text: Hay que procurar que te haga la corte un hombre que esté bien
Change to: Había que procurar ...
Changed: Había que procurar que te hiciera la corte un hombre que estuviera bien

Act One

1. *Text:* Necesito entrar sin que se entere nadie
   Change to: Necesitaba entrar ...
2. *Text:* Te escapas tres días y a la vuelta nos dices que vienes de Pamplona
   Change to: Te escapaste tres días ...
3. *Text:* Puedes llorar todo lo que quieras
   Change to: Podías llorar ...

4. *Text:* Disimulas para que no sepamos lo que sufres
   Change to: Disimulabas para que ...
5. *Text:* Aunque sea el marido no debe permitir que se escape
   Change to: Aunque fuera el marido ...
6. *Text:* Ya me arreglaré yo con lo que haya
   Change to: Ya me arreglaría yo ...
7. *Text:* No perdona que el otro sea mas feo que él
   Change to: No habría perdonado que ...
8. *Text:* Haré todo lo que digas
   Change to: Hice todo ...
9. *Text:* Me parece bien que le dés a papá una lección
   Change to: Me parecería bien ...
10. *Text:* ¿ Qué pensará su madre cuando termine aquí y vuelva a casa?
    Change to: ¿ Qué habrá pensado su madre ...

Act Two

1. *Text:* Se lo digo para que no vea que lo estoy deseando
   Change to: Se lo dije para que ...
2. *Text:* Me parece una torpeza que se pasen las tardes en El Retiro
   Change to: Me parecería una torpeza ...
3. *Text:* Tienen que verla con él para que la critiquen y se lo cuenten al tío Ricardo
   Change to: Tendrían que verla ...
4. *Text:* Hemos empezado la comedia para que el tío Ricardo tenga celos
   Change to: Habíamos empezado la comedia ...
5. *Text:* No estaré tranquilo hasta que vea cómo le suelta una bofetada
   Change to: No estuve tranquilo ...
6. *Text:* Dile que salga porque voy a matarlo
   Change to: Le dijo que ...
7. *Text:* ¿ Cree usted que hay mujer que resista lo que hace conmigo?
   Change to: ¿ Creía usted que ...
8. *Text:* ¿ Le parece cómico que yo sea el amante de su mujer?
   Change to: ¿ Le parecería cómico ...

9. *Text:* No puede concebir que su rival sea un hombre tan modesto como yo
   Change to: No podía concebir ...
10. *Text:* Estoy en el Círculo y de pronto entra un chico y me trae un recado
   Change to: Estaba en el Círculo ...

Act Three

1. *Text:* Ha ordenado que haya flores cuando él dé la lección
   Change to: Había ordenado que ...
2. *Text:* Me parece de buen gusto que él vuelva a verme así
   Change to: Me pareció de buen gusto ...
3. *Text:* Lo natural es que un marido se sienta halagado cuando su mujer gusta a otro
   Change to: Lo natural sería que ...
4. *Text:* Te has arreglado para que ese caballero te encuentre más bonita que nunca cuando entre en la casa
   Change to: Te arreglaste para que ...
5. *Text:* No es para que te des tanta importancia
   Change to: No era para que ...
6. *Text:* Ha sido una comedia para que él tenga celos de ella y vuelva a quererla
   Change to: Había sido una comedia ...
7. *Text:* Lo mejor es vivir, tomando lo que nos dé la vida
   Change to: Lo mejor sería vivir ...
8. *Text:* Espero que cuando seas mayor no juegues con los corazones
   Change to: Esperaba que ...
9. *Text:* Estoy en la broma y sé que todo es un juego
   Change to: Estaba en la broma ...
10. *Text:* Soy una pobre mujer que vive una gran aventura por primera vez
   Change to: Era una pobre mujer ...

Exercise Two: Contrasts between *Ser* and *Estar*

Directions: The expressions from the text with *ser* and *estar* in the first column may be used with either verb, but with a definite change of meaning. For each of the examples, make up a complete, original sentence, with any person and number, that will explain these subtle differences.

Expressions with Ser

EXAMPLE: Me asusta dejar de *ser joven*
Change: ... ...

1. La vida *es* muy *hermosa*
2. *Es difícil* renunciar al cariño
3. *Es mejor* que sea así
4. Las mujeres no *somos felices* a solas
5. Ese tipo de hombre siempre *es casado*
6. Claro que *eres* muy *orgullosa*
7. ¿ Para *dónde son* esas flores?
8. *Es horrible* todo esto
9. *Es muy cómodo* este sillón
10. El profesor *es* muy *amable*

Contrast with Estar

estar joven: ...
Ella *está* muy *joven* para su edad

está hermosa: ...
está difícil: ...
está mejor: ...
está feliz: ...
está casado: ...
está orgullosa: ...
¿ *Dónde está* ?: ...
está horrible: ...
está cómodo: ...
está amable: ...

Expressions with Estar

EXAMPLE: ¿ *Cómo está* el profesor?
Change: ... ...

1. El traje *está planchado*
2. Papá *está destrozado*
3. *Estás* francamente *cómico*
4. *Está enamorada* de su marido
5. *Está* muy *seguro* de ella
6. ¡ Sabes, tía, que *estás guapísima*!
7. Mamá *está* muy *nerviosa*
8. Parece que *está* algo *triste*
9. Papá no se mueve. *Está inmóvil*
10. El profesor *está listo*

Contrast with Ser

¿ *Cómo es*?: ...
Dime, ¿ *cómo es* tu novio?

es planchado (por): ...
es destrozado (por): ...
es cómico: ...
es muy *enamorado:* ...
es seguro: ...
es guapísima: ...
es nerviosa: ...
es triste: ...
es inmóvil: ...
es listo: ...

Directions: In the following expressions, only *ser* or *estar* may be used. Explain, memorize, and make up sentences with similar constructions.

Uses with Ser

1. Eso es todo
2. Es una verdadera señora
3. La verdad es otra mentira
4. ¿ Quién es ella?
5. El profesor es francés

Uses with Estar

1. Debe estar en la Universidad
2. Él ya está aquí
3. Está en el Círculo
4. Lo está recordando
5. ¿ Qué está diciendo?

6. Es verdad lo que dice
7. Es inútil
8. Es capaz de todo
9. ¿Qué es lo que ella sabe?
10. Ese es igual que tú

6. Está a tiempo
7. Está bien
8. Su vida está en peligro
9. Está harto de todo esto
10. Ella está en la broma

Exercise Three: Expressions and Idioms

Directions: Use the following expressions and idioms in complete sentences.

EXAMPLE:

Idiom: hacer caso de (alguien, algo)

Sentence: Siempre hago caso de lo que me dice mi novio (novia)

1. darse cuenta de (algo)
2. tener prisa (por)
3. tener que (+ *inf.*)
4. tener la culpa (de algo)
5. tener razón
6. tanto como
7. acabar de (+ *inf.*)
8. gustarle a (alguien)
9. saber de buena tinta
10. no poder más
11. darle (a uno) vergüenza
12. atreverse a (+ *inf.*)
13. ser capaz de (algo)
14. tratarse de (algo)
15. al parecer
16. volverse loco (por algo)
17. hacerse hombre
18. ponerse enfermo
19. a pesar de
20. sentirlo mucho (sentir ... que)
21. no se le oye (ve, etc.)
22. hay que (+ *inf.*)
23. hace un rato
24. morirse de hambre
25. tener una cita
26. quedar en (+ *inf.*)
27. tener derecho a (+ *inf.*)
28. ponerse en pie
29. ¿Qué quiere decir ... ?
30. hacer una pregunta
31. pasarse la vida (haciendo algo)
32. volver a (+ *inf.*)
33. estar de acuerdo con (alguien)
34. estar enamorado de (alguien)
35. despedirse de (alguien)
36. no decir nada (a nadie)
37. conocer (algo) (a alguien)
38. saber la lección
39. seguir hablando (leyendo, etc.)
40. ir llorando (corriendo, etc.)

Appendix:

Supplementary Techniques and Activities

In addition to the Oral Pattern Drills, the following techniques or procedures and activities are offered here as supplements for both the language and the cultural-literary aims.

I. Oral Practice through Specific Question-Answer and Completion

This type of technique is of value in fixing the correct language constructions, and follows immediately after an intensive, directed study of each page. The stress is not on the specific answer supplied, but on the construction used in both question and answer. This specific technique has the advantage of stimulating class participation, since the students ask and answer the questions.

PROCEDURE:

The instructor begins by asking the questions, but gradually trains the students themselves to formulate simple, specific questions or statements with their books open, using the constructions in the text and requiring the following type of answers:

1. A *yes* or *no* answer
2. A word or simple phrase *substitution*
3. The *completion* of the sentence with a word or phrase

The students answering the questions do so with their books closed and repeat the same phrasing as in the question, with the required, minor changes. Half of the class may ask the questions of the other half, alternating with each page, or the students who are reading the roles for that page may answer the questions asked by the other members of the class. If necessary, the instructor corrects the question before it is answered by a student.

EXAMPLES:

1. *Yes* or *no*:
   Question: Según Rosita, ¿le ha salido la barba a Manolín?
   Answer: *No*, según Rosita, *no* le ha salido la barba a Manolín
2. *Substitution*:
   Question: ¿*Qué* dice Manolín que le ha salido?
   (or) Según Manolín, ¿*qué* le ha salido?
   Answer: Manolín dice que le ha salido *la barba*
   (or) Según Manolín, le ha salido *la barba*
3. *Completion*:
   Statement: Manolín dice que le ha salido ———
   Answer: Manolín dice que le ha salido *la barba*

The stress in the above, highly simplified examples, is obviously on the construction *le ha salido* and not on the vocabulary word. Much more complicated constructions can be drilled in a similar manner.

II. General Questions, Summaries, and Topics for Discussion or Debate

INTERMEDIATE LEVEL:

With increased mastery of the language, questions can be more general and require longer answers as, for example:

Question: ¿Por qué le pregunta Tony a Rosita si están planchados sus pantalones blancos?

Answer: Tony le pregunta a Rosita si están planchados sus pantalones blancos porque tiene que estar en la Universitaria a las doce para jugar al tenis

ADVANCED LEVEL:

Advanced Spanish courses (fourth year high school or third year college level) should be able to handle controversial topics of general interest such as the following:

Problemas para discusión: pro y contra

1. Los jóvenes en *Juego de niños* hicieron bien en meterse en los asuntos de sus padres

2. La juventud española se parece mucho a la juventud norteamericana.
3. La sociedad moderna aprecia más al hombre atractivo y agresivo que al hombre tímido e idealista

III. Memorization and Dramatization of Scenes for Language Mastery

Juego de niños lends itself admirably to the memorization and dramatization of scenes because of its natural, lively dialogue and easily enacted situations. The following suggested procedure has been used extensively by the author with excellent results:

1. The play is read rapidly *in Spanish* for comprehension of the plot.

2. The acts are divided into short scenes of from three to five pages each, depending on the content and the number of students in the class, and the scenes are assigned to the members of the class.

3. The number of students assigned to any one scene depends, of course, on the characters in that scene, but the student must memorize *all the roles* in the assigned scene so that the memory work is psychologically sequential and meaningful.

4. Assigned scenes are memorized early in the quarter or semester but pronunciation and intonation should be corrected from the start.

5. Regular practice periods are provided so that the memorized scene is repeated over a long period of adequately spaced intervals.

6. The scenes, with changing roles within the group (a student should be able to perform any role in the assigned scene), are given in class as often as the time allows. A scene of three to five pages takes between six and ten minutes to perform. (An advanced Spanish Conversation class in college can easily memorize an entire act in one semester with one-page cumulative assignments.)

7. After the performance of a particular scene, members of the class can summarize, ask questions of the performers, or freely act out the same scene.

8. Professionally made tape recordings of the play for audio comprehension and student recordings for self-evaluation are invaluable aids.

9. This procedure may also be used as a preparatory technique in the selection of a cast for a full-scale student production of the play.

IV. *Juego de niños* as a Full-Scale Student Play Production

The complete version of *Juego de niños* was directed and produced by the author of this text at Stanford University with an all-American student cast. This play is unusually well adapted to student performances because of the natural, sparkling dialogue, delightful humor, amusing situations, and youthful appeal. The production also offers a minimum of technical and dramatic difficulties. The stage setting is a simple living room with sofa, chairs, a table, and lamps. There are few props and no costume problems.

The primary requirement of a successful and effective student stage production in a foreign language is complete mastery of the dialogue with proper intonation and diction. Other aesthetic considerations are necessarily secondary. With a properly selected cast, adequate direction (which need not be professional), and a minimum of three months of weekly rehearsals *after* the roles have been thoroughly memorized, the students will surely achieve the naturalness and spontaneity required for the production of *Juego de niños*. Time and spaced repetition are absolutely essential so that the memorized speech patterns, especially in a foreign language, become a natural response to a situation and not an artificial response to a word cue.

Whether the stage production of *Juego de niños* is an outgrowth of the dramatized scenes in the classroom, or a deliberately planned activity by the Spanish Club, it is sure to be a rewarding experience both from a linguistic and a literary standpoint.

V. Cultural Material for Class Discussion and Projects

Juego de niños contains many interesting references to famous artists, writers, historical figures, cities, monuments, and places of interest in Madrid. El Greco, Goya, Galdós, Felipe II, Juan de Austria, Toledo, Barcelona, Aranjuez, Sigüenza, Bilbao, Burgos, Pamplona, Palma de Mallorca, El Escorial, El Museo del Prado, and El Retiro, all constitute interesting projects of a cultural nature when combined with an adequate supply of maps of Spain and Madrid, and books on the history, geography, and customs of Spain.

Vocabulary

This vocabulary includes the words in the Spanish text and exercises except for the stated omissions. High frequency idioms are listed under the verb or the noun if not given in footnotes.

The following are omitted from the vocabulary unless special or additional meanings are involved: definite and indefinite articles; personal, reflexive, relative, and interrogative pronouns; possessive and demonstrative adjectives and pronouns; cardinal numbers under twenty; cognates identical in form and meaning (i.e., *noble*) and near cognates identical in form and meaning (i.e., *novela, estructura, paciencia, severidad, conversación*); all conjugated verb forms; regular present and past participles if no special meaning is involved; adverbs ending in *mente,* since the corresponding adjective appears, and superlatives ending in *–ísimo*; proper names needing no explanation and names of the characters in the play.

Infinitives of irregular and orthographic changing verbs (see Verb Index Table) are indicated by an asterisk (i.e., *estar**), and radical changing verbs by the corresponding basic vowel changes (i.e., *volver–ue*). The gender of nouns is not indicated for masculine nouns ending in *–o,* for feminine nouns ending in *–a, –ión, –ad, –tud, –umbre,* and for nouns with an inherent gender (i.e., *padre*).

The following abbreviations are used: *coll.* colloquial, *dim.* diminutive, *f.* feminine, *inf.* infinitive, *imperf.* imperfect, *m.* masculine, *n.* noun, *p.p.* past participle, *pres.* present, and *pres. part.* present participle.

A

a to; at, on, in; by; after; **te diriges — Rosita** (not translated as a personal **a**); **y — beber** and let's drink
abajo below, under
abandonado abandoned; **está muy —** (he) is very lonely
abandonar to abandon; **tener abandonado a alguien** to neglect someone
abatido discouraged, dejected
abierto open, generous; *p.p.* of **abrir** opened; **con los ojos bien abiertos** with his eyes wide open
abogado lawyer
abrazar* to embrace, hug; **abrazarse a** to hug
abrir to open
abrumado crushed; overwhelmed
aburrirse to be bored, become bored
abusar to go too far; to take undue advantage (of another)
abuso abuse; a deceitful act
acabar to finish, end; **— de** (+ *inf.*) (used in *pres.* and *imperf.*) to have just
acariciar to caress, fondle; to comfort
acatarrarse to catch a cold
acento accent; intonation
aceptar to accept
acercarse* a to go near, go up to, approach
acometer to attack; to overtake; **le acometió el sueño** he fell asleep
acometido attacked; **— de** struck by (an idea)
acompañar to accompany
acordarse (ue) de to remember, think of
acostar (ue) to put to bed; **acostarse** to go to bed, lie down
acostumbrar(se) to get used to
acotación directions
actitud attitude
acto act (of a play); action
acudir to go, come (to the rescue); to rush up (to someone)
acuerdo accord, agreement; **estar de —** to agree; to conspire
ademán *m.* gesture, look
además moreover, besides
adiós good-bye
adivinar to guess, divine
admirar to admire
adolescente adolescent; *n., m.* and *f.* teen-ager
adónde where
adquirir (ie) to acquire, obtain, get
adulterio adultery
advertir (ie) to notice, observe; to advise, give notice or warning
afectuoso affectionate
afeitarse to shave
aficionado fond (of)
afuera out, outside; **las afueras** the outskirts, suburbs
agotar to exhaust
agradable agreeable, pleasant
agradecer* to acknowledge; to show gratitude
agradecido grateful
¡ah! ah! alas!; oh!; **¡ah, bueno!** oh, come now! (used sarcastically)
ahí there
ahogado smothered, stifled
ahogar* to drown, stifle
ahora now; **de —** of today; **— mismo** just now, right now
airado angry; **mirando airadamente** glaring at
aire *m.* air; **se da —** fans himself
ajeno another's
al = a + el to the; **—** (+ *inf.*) on, upon; **—** (+ *pres. part.*) when as,
ala *f.* wing; **dar alas** to give wings (i.e., freedom)
alborotarse to become excited, become agitated
alboroto agitation, excitement
alborozado gay, joyful, excited
alborozo excitement
alegrarse (de) to be glad (of)
alegre gay, pleasing; happy
alejado withdrawn; separated
alentador encouraging
alfombra rug
algazara din, clamor, noise
algo something; somewhat, a little
alguien someone

alguno (**algún**) some, any; **algunos** a few, some; **algunas veces** some times
alma soul; **querer con toda el —** to love with all one's heart
alternativo alternate
altivez *f.* haughtiness, pride
alzar* to raise; **— los ojos** to look up
allá there; back there
allí there
amable kind, amiable, courteous, obliging
amada the beloved, the one loved
amante *m.* or *f.* mistress, lover
amar to love
amargo bitter
amargura bitterness
ambiente *m.* atmosphere
amigo friend
amilanarse to become terrified; to become discouraged
amonestar to admonish, advise
amor *m.* love
amoroso loving
ancho wide; **a sus anchas** in comfort; nonchalantly
andanzas adventures
andar* to walk; to go, move; **¡ anda!** well! really! come now!; **anda por aquí** he's around here
anécdota anecdote
ángel angel; **tener —** to be charming, attractive
angustia anguish
angustiado grieved, worried, anxious
anoche last night
anonadado crushed, overwhelmed
anónimo anonymous note or letter; **— amoroso** anonymous love note
anotar to comment (on)
ansiedad anxiety
ante in front of; before
antepecho balcony
anterior previous, preceding
antes before, formerly; **— de** (+ *inf.*) before; **— (de) que** before; rather than
anticuado antiquated, old-fashioned
antiguo ancient, old; **Madrid —** the old section of Madrid from the *Puerta del Sol* to the *Palacio*
antipático displeasing, obnoxious
año year
apagar* to put out; to turn off (lights)
aparecer* to appear, show up
apariencia appearance
apasionado passionate; with deep emotion
apegado attached
apenas hardly, scarcely
apesadumbrado sad, grief-stricken
aplaudir to applaud
apoyado leaning
apreciar to appreciate
aprender to learn
apresurado hurried
aprisa swiftly, quickly
aprovechar to profit by; make use of; **aprovecharse de** to take advantage of; to annoy; **que no se aproveche** he must not take advantage (of it)
apurado worried
aquí here; **— estoy** here I am
Aranjuez a town south of Madrid, famous for its Royal Palace, a favorite residence of the kings of Spain
árbol *m.* tree
ardor *m.* ardor, dash, courage
arquitecto architect
arrancar* to pull out
arrebato fit, sudden vehemence
arreglar to arrange, settle; **arreglarse** to fix, make up; **— matrimonios** to patch up difficulties between married couples
arreglo arrangement
arrepentirse (**ie**) to repent; to change one's mind
arriba above; **de — abajo** from top to bottom, up and down
arrodillarse to kneel down
asegurar to assure
asesino assassin, murderer
así so, thus, that way, like that; **¡ — estudia usted!** so that's the way you study!

asistir (**a**) to attend, to be present at
asomar to appear
asombrado astonished
asombrar to astonish
asombroso astonishing
aspecto aspect, look; **no tener buen** — to look ill, tired
asunto matter; affair
asustado frightened
asustar to frighten; **asustarse** to be frightened
atardecer *m.* late afternoon
atención attention, interest
atento attentive
aterrado terrified, appalled
¡ atiza ! (*coll.*) golly! (euphemism suggesting something stronger)
atizar* to stir the fire with a poker; (*coll.*) to poke (someone)
atónito astonished, amazed
atraer* to attract
atravesar (**ie**) to cross, cross over
atreverse (**a**) to dare
atrevido daring, bold
audaz bold, fearless
aun (**aún**) even; still, yet
aunque although, even though
auricular *m.* headphone, receiver
ausencia absence
ausente absent
auténtico authentic; real
autorizar* to authorize
avanzar* to advance, come forward
avergonzado ashamed
averiguar* to investigate
Ávila a mediaeval, walled city W. by N. of Madrid. The birthplace of Saint Theresa
¡ ay ! oh! oh goodness! ouch!
ayer yesterday
azarado confused, rattled
azararse to become rattled, confused
azorado bewildered
azul blue

B

bailar to dance; **¡ a — !** let us dance!
bajar to descend, get off; lower; — **los ojos** to look down
bajo under, beneath; low, mean; **de bajos fondos** cheap; **bajito** in a whisper
balcón *m.* balcony
bandeja tray; **bandejita** small tray
baño bath; **cuarto de** — bathroom
barato cheap, inexpensive; **baratita** cheapish
barba beard; chin; **salir**(**le**) **la** — to start growing a beard
barbaridad atrocity; blunder; nonsense; **¡ qué — !** good heavens! how dreadful!; **una** — an awful lot; **decir barbaridades** to talk nonsense
barca small boat
Barcelona the most important manufacturing and trading city in Spain, located on the northeastern coast
barrio district, quarter, suburb
bastante enough, sufficient; quite
bastar to be enough, suffice; **¡ basta!** that will do!; stop!; **¿ no basta mi palabra?** isn't my word enough?
bata dressing gown, bathrobe
beber to drink
belleza beauty
bello beautiful
benévolo kind, gentle
besar to kiss
beso kiss
bien well, all right; **muy** — very well; **está** — all right; **un hombre que esté** — (i.e.) a gentleman
Bilbao a highly industrial Basque town and one of Spain's main seaports
birria (*coll.*) a "square"; a "fool"
blanco white; **de punta en** — in full regalia, all dressed up
boca mouth; — **de fresa** "ruby" lips
bofetada slap in the face
"**boîte**" (*French*) cabaret, night club
bolsillo pocket
bondadoso kind; **con** —(**a**) **reconvención** gently reproachful
bonito pretty; **sería tan** — it would be so pleasant

boquiabierto open-mouthed; astonished
botella bottle
boxear to box
¡ bravo! bravo! hurrah!
brazo arm
brillar to shine
brinco leap, jump
brocha brush; — **de afeitar** shaving brush
broma joke; practical joke
bronca (*coll.*) fight
brusco rude; sudden, harsh
bruto brutish, beastly; *n., m.* brute; **brutote** you big brute
búcaro small flower vase
bueno good; all right; well; **¡ ah, —!** oh, come now!
Burgos capital of the province of Burgos, of great historical and architectural interest, especially noted for its cathedral
buscar* to search, look for, seek; — **con los ojos** to look around

C

¡ ca ! oh, no!; no, indeed!
caballeresco chivalrous
caballero gentleman; sir
caber* to fit
cabeza head; **mover la** — to shake one's head
cabo end; **al — de** at the end of
cacharro piece of crockery
cada each, every; **uno a — lado** one at each side
caer* to fall; **se le cae . . .** (he) drops . . .; — **bien** to like, find (someone) charming
café *m.* coffee; "café"
caliente warm, hot
calmoso calm(ly); slow(ly)
callado silent
callar to be silent; to hush; **callarse** to stop talking; **callárselo** to keep it to oneself; **¡ que te calles!** I told you to keep quiet! shut up!
calle *f.* street; **callecita** little (narrow) street
cama bed
cambiar to change; exchange; **¡ Voy a — de vida!** I'm going to change my way of life!
cambio change; **en** — on the other hand
camino road, path, way; — **de** on the way to, in the direction of
camisa shirt
campanada stroke of a bell or clock
cana gray hair
canalla *m.* scoundrel
canción song; — **del día** a song in vogue
cansado tired
cansar to tire, weary; **cansarse** (**de**) to become tired or weary
capaz capable; **ser — de** to be capable of, have the courage to
Capitol *m.* a movie house in Madrid on the "Gran vía"
capricho whim, fancy
cara face
¡ caramba ! (*coll.*) darn it!; well, I'll be darned!; no!!; gosh!
carantoña caress; **carantoñas** soft words of endearment
¡ caray ! (*coll.*) **¡ caramba !** gosh!
carcajada burst of laughter; **prorrumpir en carcajadas** to burst out laughing
carecer* to lack
cargado full; (*coll.*) vexed, annoyed; — **de razón** confident of being right
cariño affection, love
cariñoso affectionate
caro expensive
carretera road, highway
carta letter; card; **jugar a las cartas** to play cards
casa house, home; **en** — at home; **a** — home
casado married; *n.* married man; **una de esas casadas** one of those married women
casarse to marry
casi almost
castellano Castilian (Spanish language)

catedral *f.* cathedral (i.e., the main cathedral of a city is *la Catedral*)
causa cause; reason
cautela caution
cejijunto frowning (the word combines *junto* = near and *cejas* = eyebrows)
celo ardor, zeal; **celos** jealousy; **tener celos** to be jealous; **dar celos (a alguien)** to make (someone) jealous
cenar to dine, have dinner
centro center, middle
ceñudo frowning; gruff
cerca near
cerrar (ie) to close, shut
cielo sky, heaven; — **mío** my dear, my darling
ciento (short form *cien*) one hundred; **por** — per cent
cierto certain, a certain; sure; **ser** — to be true
cigarrillo cigarette
cine *m.* cinema, "movie"; movies
Círculo (el) the Club, Casino
cita date, appointment
citar to make an appointment; **estar citado(s)** to have an appointment
ciudad city; — **de derecha** a conservative or straight-laced city
ciudadano citizen
claro clear; of course, to be sure; **¡claro!** naturally!; **¡— que sí!** yes indeed! of course! to be sure!
clase *f.* class; kind; lesson
clavar to nail; — **los ojos** to stare (at)
cobarde *m.* coward
coche *m.* car; — **de línea** direct bus or train service
cocina kitchen
"**cóckteles**" *m.* (*Anglicism*) cocktail parties
coger* to take, seize, catch; to pick up
colegiala college girl
colgar* (ue) to hang, hang up
colmo end, limit; **¡es el —!** that's the limit!
colosal colossal, terrific
collar *m.* necklace; collar
comedia comedy; play; **hacer la** — to play act, put on an act
comenzar* (ie) a to begin, start
comer to eat
cómico comical; ludicrous, ridiculous
como as, like, in the same manner as; since; — **si** as if; — **siempre** as usual; — **no** of course; **¿cómo?** how? **¿cómo que ah, bueno?** what do you mean "oh, come now!"
cómodo comfortable; convenient; **ponerse** — to make oneself comfortable
compadecer* to pity
compasión compassion, pity; **tener — de** to pity
complacido pleased
complejo complex
completo complete; **por** — completely, altogether
componer* to fix, adjust
comprar to buy, purchase
comprender to understand; to realize; to include; **ya se comprende** that's obvious
con with
concebir (i) to conceive; to understand
concierto concert; "concerto" (in music)
conciliador conciliatory; appeasing (ly)
condición condition, quality; **condiciones** qualifications; **estar en** — to be qualified
conducir* to conduct, lead
confianza confidence, trust
confiar to hope, trust
confidencia trust, confidence; **hacer confidencias** to confide
confidencial confidential; confidentially
conflicto conflict, difficulty
confundido bewildered, confused
confuso confused, perplexed
conmovido affected, moved
conocer* to know; to be or become acquainted with; to meet

conque so then, and so
conquistar to conquer; to win another's affections
considerar to consider
consolador consoling
constar (used impersonally) to be evident, clear; to note; **conste que** it should be clear that
construir* to construct, build, make
contar (**ue**) to tell, relate; to confide; — **con** to depend on; **cuentan y no acaban** (they) never stop talking about it; **¡ cuéntamelo !** tell me about it!
contemplar to contemplate, observe
contemporáneo contemporary
contener* to contain
contenido restrained; controlled
contento pleased, satisfied
contestar to answer
continuar* to continue, follow
continuo continuous
¡ contra ! (*coll.*) darn it! (a euphemism for a stronger expression)
contrariado disappointed; vexed
contrario contrary; **lo** — the contrary; **llevar la contraria** to contradict
contratar to deal; to plan
contribuir* to contribute
convalecencia convalescence; restfulness (after excitement)
convencer* to convince; **convencerse de** to convince oneself of
convenir* to suit; to agree
convertir (**ie**) to convert, transform, change; **convertirse en** to become
copiar to copy
coqueta flirt
coquetear to flirt
coquetería coquetry
coraje *m.* anger; courage; **con** — angrily
corazón *m.* heart
corbata tie
coronilla small crown; top of the head; **andar de** — to do something diligently; (*coll.*) to be kept hopping
correcto correct, proper; **lo** — what is proper, just enough
corregir* to correct
correr to run
corresponder to correspond; to befit
corrigiendo correcting
corte *f.* court; courtship; **hacer la** — to court, make love to
cortés courteous, polite
cosa thing; matter; **poca** — insignificant (thing or person); **¡ psché ! cosas** oh, just somewhere, just doing things
costar (**ue**) to cost
costumbre custom, habit; **tener** — to be accustomed to
crecer* to grow
creer* to believe, think; **¿ tú crees?** do you really think so?; **creo que sí** I think so
creyendo believing
criado (*p.p.* of *criar*) brought up; **mal** — spoiled; *n.*, *m.* or *f.* servant
crimen *m.* crime
crisis *f.* crisis; nervous crisis
cristal *m.* glass
cristalera glass partition
cristiano Christian
criticar* to criticize
"**croissant**" (*French*) bun, roll
cruzar* to cross; **se cruzan sus miradas** their glances (eyes) meet
cuadro picture, painting
cualquier(**a**) any, anyone, anybody; **un cualquiera** a nobody
cuando when; on the occasion of
cuanto as much as, whatever; **unos cuantos** a few
cuarenta forty
cuarto room; — **de baño** bathroom; — **de estudio** study
cucharilla teaspoon
cuchichear to whisper; **cuchicheo** whispering
cuello neck; collar; **con la toalla al** — with the towel around his neck
cuenta account, bill; **darse** — to notice, realize, be aware of; **¿ te das —?** have you noticed?
cuento story, tale

cuestión question; matter
cueva cave; **cuevas de Drach** (*see* Drach)
cuidar to take care of, care for
culpa blame, guilt; **tener la —** to be to blame; **no es mía la —** it's not my fault; **por su —** on your account
cumplidor *m.* reliable
cumplir to perform, fulfill; **— con** to fulfill (one's obligation); **por —** as a matter of form
curiosidad curiosity
curioso curious, strange; **es —** it's interesting

CH

champán: champaña *m.* champagne
chasqueado disappointed
chico little, small; *n., m.* lad, youngster, dear boy; **chiquillo** (*dim.*) child, kid; **pero chiquilla** but my dear child
chiflado (*coll.*) to become mentally unbalanced, crazy; **están chifladas por él** they (the girls) are crazy about him
chiflar to whistle; **me chiflan** (*coll.*) I'm crazy about them
chillar to scream
¡ chist ! hush! quiet!; **¡ chisss !** quiet! hey!
chivato kid; (*coll.*) kid brother
chocar* to strike, hit; (*coll.*) **¡ chóquela!** (shake hands)!
chocolatería hot chocolate stand; **— de bajos fondos** a "typical" and inexpensive type of hot chocolate "bar" in the old section of Madrid

D

daño hurt, injury; **hacer —** to hurt, injure
dar* to give; to strike; **¡ y dale!** there you go again!; **— puntapiés** to kick; **darse aires** to put on airs; **darle rabia a alguien** to make someone furious
de of, from; because of; by; **— fiesta en fiesta** from one party to another
deber to have to; must, should, ought to; *n., m.* duty
débil weak
decente decent; honest; nice; proper, well-behaved
decepción disappointment
decidido decided
decidir to decide, determine; **decidirse a** to make up one's mind to
decir* to say, tell; to state; **querer —** to mean, signify; **¡ no me diga!** you don't say!
declamar to declame
declaración declaration (of love), vow of love; **— de amor** proposal, confession of one's love
declararse to propose; to express or confess one's love for another
decorado decoration; set, scenery
decoro decency; honor, respect for others
defender (ie) to defend
dejar to leave, give up; to let, allow, permit; **— de** to stop, fail to, cease; **— de ser joven** to lose (one's) youth; **dejarse** to let, allow oneself; **deje, deje ...** it's all right, let it be ...
delicado delicate, gentle; sensitive
delicioso delightful
demasiado too much; excessively
denotar to denote; to explain
dentro inside
derecho right; **a la derecha** on the right hand; **de derecha** conservative
desahogar* to relieve pain; **desahogarse** to express one's feelings, get rid of one's frustrations
desaliento discouragement
desaliñado neglectful, slovenly
desaliño negligence, slovenliness
desaparecer* to disappear
desayunar (se) to breakfast, have breakfast
desayuno breakfast
descalzar* (se) to take off (one's) shoes or stockings

descansar to rest
descarado impudent; shameless; *n.* shameless one
descompuesto out of order; **todo —** completely upset
desconcertado confused
desconfiado distrustful
desconocido unknown (person)
desconsolado disconsolate, unhappy
desconsuelo affliction; **con —** grieved, with grief
descubierto discovered
descubrir to discover; to reveal
desde from; since; **— luego** of course; **— hace un rato** for quite a while; **— mañana** starting tomorrow
desdén *m.* disdain, scorn, contempt
desear to desire, wish, want
desesperación despair
desesperado in despair
desesperar to lose hope, despair
desgraciado miserable, unhappy; *n.* wretch; **soy un —** I'm a miserable wretch
desnudo nude, naked
desolado desolate; in despair
despacio slowly; **despacito** very slowly
despacho study
desparpajo boldness; **con —** boldly
despedir (**i**) to dismiss; **despedirse de** to take leave, say good-bye
despertar(**se**) (**ie**) to awaken
despistar to mislead, sidetrack; to throw one off the right trail
despiste (*coll.*) *m.* wrong track; **¡ qué — !** how stupid of me!
después after, afterwards; then, later; **— de** after; **— de todo** after all
destino destiny, fate
destrozado shattered; (*coll.*) done in
destrozar* to destroy
desvergüenza impudence, shamelessness
detalle *m.* detail
detenerse* to stop, be detained
detrás de behind, back of
devolver (**ue**) to return (someone or something)
día *m.* day; **de —** during the day, day time; **hacerse de —** to become daylight; **¡ qué — !** what a day!; **buenos días** good morning; **todos los días** every day
diabólico diabolical, devilish
diario daily
diciendo saying
dictar to dictate
dicho said, told
dichoso happy
Dieu (*French*) God; **"Oh, mon —!"** oh, dear God!
difícil difficult
dignidad dignity
digno worthy; **muy —** or **con dignidad** with (forced) dignity; **con dignísima amargura** with bitterly hurt dignity
dinero money
dintel *m.* doorhead
Dios *m.* God; **¡ — mío !** for heaven's sake!; **¡ por — !** for goodness sake!
dirigir* (**se**) **a** to direct oneself to; to address; to turn to
discreción discretion, prudence
disculparse de to excuse oneself, apologize, give excuses
disgustado disgusted; annoyed
disgusto disgust; annoyance
disimular to pretend, feign; to conceal (one's feelings)
disimulo pretense; **con —** on the sly, furtively, unobserved
disminuir* to diminish, lessen
disparate *m.* blunder; a rash act; **hacer un —** to do something foolish
disponer* to dispose; to get ready; **disponerse a** to get ready to
dispuesto ready
distante distant, remote, far
distinguido distinguished
distinguir* to distinguish
divertido amused
divertir (**ie**) to amuse; **divertirse** to have a good time
divirtiendo amusing

doblado folded
doble double; — **sentido** double meaning
dolido hurt
doloroso painful
domingo Sunday; **los domingos** on Sundays
doncella maid, servant
donde where; **por** — through which; **¿ (a) dónde ?** where?
doña title of respect used before a woman's Christian name only
dormir (ue) to sleep, go to sleep; **dormirse** to fall asleep
Drach, cuevas de caves near Manacor in Mallorca, famous for their stalactites and underground lakes
duda doubt
dudar to doubt; — **de** to distrust
duende *m.* elf, goblin, ghost
dulce sweet
duquesa duchess
durante during; for
durar to last
durmiente *m.* sleeping (boy)

E

¡ ea! come, come!; so there! (an interjection to attract attention)
eco echo
echado thrown, cast; lying down; **el toldo está** — the awning is down
echar to throw, cast, toss; to throw out; **echarse a** to begin to, start
edad age; period
educación education; good breeding, politeness; **mala** — bad manners
educar* to educate; to train, raise, bring up
efusivo effusive, enthusiastic
egoísta selfish, egoistic
¿ eh? huh? isn't that so?
ejemplar *m.* copy
embargado seized
embargo: sin — however, nevertheless
embustero liar, hypocrite; **¡ qué —!** what a liar! what a fibber!
emocionado deeply moved; **mirada emocionada** affectionate look
emocionante touching, moving; **¡será —!** it will be terrific!
emocionarse to be moved, thrilled
empeñarse en to persist; to insist stubbornly
empezar* (ie) a to begin
empinado steep
en in, into; at; on, upon
enamorado loving, in love; — **de** in love with; *n.* one in love
enamorar to make love (to someone); **enamorarse de** to fall in love
enardecido fired with enthusiasm
encantado charmed, delightful
encantador charming, delightful
encanto delight; darling (used as a term of endearment); **un — de calamidad** a delightful calamity
encargar* to order; **encargarse de** to take charge of, to see to
encontrar (ue) to find; **encontrarse (a) (con)** to meet, encounter
energía energy, vigor
enérgico forceful
energúmeno person possessed of the devil; **como un** — fighting mad
enfadado angry, vexed
enfermedad illness
enfermo ill
engañar to deceive
enhorabuena congratulation(s)
enjabonado soapy; covered with soap
enojo anger
enorme enormous, tremendous
enrojecer* to blush
ensayar to try, practice
enseñar a to teach; to show, point out
ensimismado absorbed in thought
entender (ie) to understand
enterar to inform, let know; **enterarse de** to discover, find out
enternecido touched, moved to pity
entonces then; well then; at that time
entrada entrance, door
entrar to enter; — **en** to go in (into)
entre between; among; in

entretener* to amuse, entertain; to delay
entusiasmado enthused; excited
entusiasmo enthusiasm
enviar* to send
envidiar to envy
envolver (**ue**) to wrap; to envelop, enfold
equivocar* to mistake; **equivocarse** to make a mistake, be mistaken
equívoco misunderstanding
erguir* (**ie** = **ye**) to raise; **erguirse** to straighten up
escalofrío chill; shudder; **me producen escalofríos** (they) terrify me
escamado irritated, resentful, offended
escandalizado scandalized
escándalo scandal; **¡ qué — !** how scandalous!
escaparse to escape; to run off
escena stage; scene; **en —** on stage; **hacer una —** to make a scene
esclavo slave
escoger* to choose, select
Escorial (**El**) an enormous building near Madrid built between 1563–1584 by Philip II
escribir to write
escrúpulo scruple
escuchar to listen, listen to
escuela school; **la vieja —** the old-fashioned school
espalda back; shoulders; **vuelta de espaldas** her back turned; **volver la —** to turn one's back
espanto fright, terror
espantoso frightful, dreadful
español Spanish; **el —** Spanish (language); Spaniard
esperanza hope; encouragement
esperar to expect; to hope; to wait (for)
esposa wife
esquina corner
establecido established
estadística statistics
estallar to explode
estancia sitting room, living room
estar* to be; **estése usted quieto** behave yourself; **está bien** it's all right
éste (**ésta**) the latter
estentóreamente very loudly
estilo style; **por el —** of that sort
estimular to stimulate, encourage
estirar to stretch; to pull
estrechar to tighten; to press; **— la mano** to shake hands
estrecho narrow
estrenar to do for the first time; **— tres sombreros** to put on three new hats
estreno début; first performance
estropear to spoil, ruin
estudiar to study
estudio study; **cuarto de —** study, studio
estupefacto motionless, astonished
estupendo stupendous, terrific
estúpido stupid; **¡ estúpida !** you stupid little fool!
evidente evident; obvious
evitar to avoid
exagerar to exaggerate
exaltarse to get excited, upset
examen *m.* examination
examinar to examine
excitado excited
exigente demanding, hard to please
éxito success
explicación explanation
explicar* to explain; **no me lo explico** I can't understand it
explícito explicit, clear
extendido extended, outstretched
extranjero foreigner
extrañar to surprise; to find strange; to wonder at
extrañeza surprise
extraño strange
extremo end

F

fácil easy
facha (*coll.*) appearance; look; face; (**él**) **no tiene mala —** he isn't bad looking

falta fault; lack; mistake
faltar to be lacking; be wanting; to offend, insult; — **al respeto** to treat (someone) disrespectfully; **¡no faltaría más** of course (not)!
fallar to fail; to miss
familiar familiar; domestic, homelike
farsante *m.* fraud, pretender
fatalidad fatality, calamity; fate
favor *m.* favor; **por** — please
favorecer* to favor; to flatter
felicidad happiness
felicitación (*pl.* **felicitaciones**) congratulations
felicitar to congratulate
feliz happy; **estar** — to be overjoyed
feo ugly
fiarse to trust
fiebre *f.* fever
fiesta party, social event; **de — en —** from party to party
figura figure, shape; appearance
figurar to appear, be (i.e., on a list); **figurarse** to imagine
fijamente intensely; fixedly; **mirar** — to stare
fijarse to notice
fin *m.* end; purpose, object; **buen** — good intentions; **al** — finally, after all; **en** — finally; well ... (used as an expletive)
final *m.* end
fingir* to pretend, feign
fino courteous, polite
firmar to sign
fiscal fiscal; prosecutor-like; (*coll.*) censuring
flamante bright, sparkling
flamenco (*coll.*) fresh **¡no seas flamenca!** don't be fresh (or bold)
"**flirt**" "flirtation"; **fingir un** — to pretend to carry on a flirtation
flirtear (*Anglicism*) to flirt
flor *f.* flower
fondo background; backstage; bottom; fund; **al** — in the background, backstage; **a** — perfectly, thoroughly; **en el** — at bottom, in reality, at heart; **de bajos fondos** inexpensive (i.e., of low funds)
formal serious, proper; formal
fortuna fortune, (good) luck
fotografía picture, photograph
fracasar to fail
francés French; **el** — French (language), Frenchman
franco frank, open; **francamente** decidedly
frasco flask, bottle, vase
frase *f.* phrase; expression; **con su última** — with (her) last words
frente in front of, opposite
fresa strawberry
fresco fresh, cheeky, forward; **un** — a cheeky or fresh person
frío cold
frivolidad frivolity
Fuentecilla a small fountain in the old part of Madrid
fuera out, outside; — **de** out of; **comer — de casa** to eat out; **¡—!** out of here!
fuerte strong; loud
fuerza force; strength; **fuerzas** strength
fumar to smoke
furia fury
furioso furious; **con furiosísimo orgullo** with extreme pride

G

gabardina coat
galantería gallantry
gana wish, desire; **las ganas** ... you'd like that ...
ganar to win
ganga bargain
garaje *m.* garage
gastar to spend; to waste; — **una broma** to play a joke
genio temper; **geniecito** (*coll.*) bad temper (*dim.* used ironically)
gente *f.* people
gesto gesture; look
golfo (*coll.*) rascal, rake, libertine
golpe *m.* blow; **golpecito** pat

Goya, Francisco de (1746–1828) a famous Spanish painter whose portraits of the Spanish life of his times are unequalled
gozoso joyful
gracia grace; cleverness; **¿ no tiene — ?** isn't it funny?; **te hacen —** you are amused by; **dar las gracias** to thank; **a Dios gracias** thank goodness
gracioso graceful; amusing, funny; **lo — es** the amusing thing is
grande (**gran**) big, large; great
granuja *m.* (*coll.*) rogue, rascal; **¡ qué — !** what a rascal!
grave serious
Greco (El): Domenico Theotocopuli (1542–1614) famous Spanish painter of Greek origin, who settled in Toledo. His elongated figures have some of the characteristics of modern art
gripe *f.* grippe; influenza ("flu"); **pescar una —** to catch or come down with the "flu"
gritar to shout, yell, cry out
grito cry, shout; **en un —** at the top of (his) voice; **dar un —** to shout; **pegar un —** to scream
gruñir* to growl, grunt; to grumble
guante *m.* glove
guapo good-looking, handsome
guateque (*coll.*) wild party
guía guide; **— turística** tourist guide
gustar to please; to like; to prefer; **— de** to have a liking for; **me gustaría** I would like, prefer; **¿ os gusto?** do you like me?
gusto pleasure; **a tu —** as you please; **de buen —** in good taste

H

haber* to have (*auxiliary*); to be (*impersonal*); **— de** to need to, have to, must; **hay** there is, there are; **hay que** it it necessary
habitación room, dwelling
habitar to inhabit, reside
hablar to speak
hacer* to do; to make; to be; **— gracia** to amuse; **— la comedia** to put on an act; **— una visita** to pay a visit; **— un viaje** to take a trip; **— confidencias** to confide; **— preguntas** to ask questions; **— bien en** to be justified in; **hacerse** to become
hacia toward, to; about; **— aquí** this way
halagar* to flatter
hallar to find; **hallarse** to be, be located
hallazgo finding, discovery
hambre *f.* hunger
harto full, complete, satiated; **estar —** to be fed up
hasta even; until, up to, as far as
hecho done; made; **— un lío** all mixed up
herir (**ie**) to wound; **francamente herido** quite obviously hurt
hermana sister
hermano brother; **primos hermanos** first cousins
hermoso beautiful
hija daughter; **¡ — !** my child! my dear! my dear girl!
hijo son; **¡ — !** my boy! my dear boy! my dear!; **los hijos** children
hipofosfito hypophosphite (an emulsion with cod-liver oil)
historia history; tale, story
hito fixed; **mirar de — en —** to stare at (someone)
hogar *m.* home; hearth
hojear to read over hastily; glance at
¡ hola ! hello!; well!
hombre man; **¡ —!** (*coll.*) look here!; **¡— no!** good heavens, no!; **un pobre —** a poor devil; **— de mundo** a man of the world, of experience; **¡ hola, — !** hello, there!
homenaje *m.* homage; high compliment
hondo deep
hora hour
horrible horrible, horrid; **tener celos horribles** to be horribly jealous

horror *m.* horror; **¡ qué —!** how dreadful!
horrorizado horrified
hoy today
huir* to flee, run away
¡ hum ! hmm ...; huh!
humildad humility
humilde humble
humillado humiliated
humillar to humiliate
humor *m.* disposition, temper; — **pésimo** ill-tempered
hundir to sink; to bury; **hundirse** to be ruined, destroyed
huraño shy; intractable
¡ huy! oh, dear!; oh!
huyendo fleeing

I

idealista idealistic (for both masculine and feminine nouns)
idioma *m.* language, tongue
idiota *m.* idiot, fool
ignorante ignorant; *n.*, *m.* or *f.* **un** (**una**) — an ignoramus
ignorar to be ignorant of, not to know; to ignore
igual equal, the same; **ser — a** to be identical, exactly like (someone)
iluminado enlightened; inspired (by an idea)
ilusión illusion; **con —** with excitement
ilustre famous, distinguished
imitar to imitate
impedir (**i**) **a** to prevent
ímpetu *m.* impetus, impulse; abandon
imponente imposing; **¡ — !** terrific!; (*coll.*) **estar —** to look terrific
importancia importance; **tener —** to be important
importar to be important; to matter; **no** (**me**) **importa** it's no concern (of mine); **si no te importa** if you don't mind
impresionado impressed; disturbed
impresionante impressive, astonishing
inadvertido unnoticed
incontenible uncontrollable
inconveniente *m.* objection; drawback; **tener —** to object
incorporarse to sit up
increíble incredible
indignado indignant, offended
individuo fellow; (*coll.*) **ese —** that "character"
indudable certain, unquestionable
infiel unfaithful
infierno hell
ingenuo candid; naïve
inglesa English woman
inmóvil motionless, fixed; frozen
inocente innocent; **¡ es más —!** she's so innocent!
inquieto worried
inquirir (**ie**) to inquire, look into
insensato fool, stupid fool
insinuar to insinuate; suggest
instalado set up, installed
instante *m.* instant, moment; **al —** immediately
intención intention, purpose; **sin mala —** without malice
intentar to attempt, try
interés *m.* interest
interesado interested
interesante interesting
interpretar to interpret
interrumpir to interrupt
íntimo intimate
inútil useless, of no use
inventar to invent, make up
invitar to invite
ir* to go; to be, to get along; **— a** (+ *inf.*) to go to, be about to; **irse** to go, go away; **irse de viaje** to go off on a trip; **¡ vamos !** well! come now!; **va transformándose en** (it) gradually becomes
ironía irony
irritar to irritate
irrumpir to "burst" in
izquierda left

J

jamás ever, never
jardín *m.* garden
jaula cage

¡je! huh! uh ... (a kind of "grunt" to indicate embarrassment)
Josefina Josephine, the wife of Napoleon Bonaparte
joven young; *n.*, *m.* youth, young man; *n.*, *f.* young woman; **jóvenes** young people
jovial gay
júbilo joy, glee, happiness
jubiloso joyful
juego game; **estar en el —** to conspire in, be "in on" the game
juerga (*coll.*) spree, wild party; **de —** out on a spree
jugador *m.* player
jugar* (**ue**) to play; to gamble
juguete *m.* toy
junto near; **— a** next to, by; **juntos** together
jurar to swear
justo just, correct, exact; **tiempo —** exact time
juzgar* to judge; to pass or render judgment (on); **— mal** to misjudge, judge harshly

L

labio lip
lado side
lagartona tricky (or foxy) woman (a term used to show contempt)
lágrima tear
lanzar* throw, hurl, fling; **— un grito** to cry out, scream; **lanzarse** to fling oneself
largo long; **puesta de —** coming out party
lástima pity; **tener — de alguien** to be sorry for someone
lateral lateral; from the side
lección lesson
leche *f.* milk
leer* to read
legalizar* to legalize, authorize
lejano distant, far away
lejos far; **— de** far from; **desde —** from a distance
lento slow
levantar to raise; to lift; to build; **levantarse** to get up, arise
leve light; slight; brief; **una pausa levísima** a very brief pause
ley *f.* law
leyenda legend
leyendo reading
libro book
limpieza cleaning
lindo pretty; lovely
línea line; **coche de —** direct bus or train line
lío intrigue; scrape; affair; (*coll.*) **hecho un —** completely confused
listo ready; quick; **ser —** to be smart, clever
lo it, him; **— de** about; the matter of; **— de siempre** as usual; **— que** what; how; how much; **— que ocurre** the trouble is; **— que pasa** what happens
loco crazy; **me tienes —** I'm mad about you; **volverse —** to go out of one's mind; **enamorado como un —** madly in love
locura madness
luego soon; then, presently, at once; later; **desde —** to be sure
lugar *m.* place
lujo elegance; **de —** de luxe
lujoso elegant, luxurious
luna moon; **en la —** in the clouds
luz *f.* light; **luces** lights

LL

llamar to call; to attract; to call out; **¿me llaman?** is someone calling me?
llegar* to arrive; to approach; **— a** (+ *inf.*) to succeed in, come to
lleno full, filled
llevar* to carry; to take; to wear; **— la contraria** to contradict
llorar to cry

M

"madame" (*French*) madam; **"oh, madame!"** oh, my dear lady!
madre mother

Madrid capital of Spain with a population of about two million; **el antiguo** — the old section of the city from Puerta del Sol to the Palacio, of both historical and architectural interest
madrugada dawn; early morning; **anoche de** — late last night (i.e., early this morning)
madrugar* to rise early
mal badly; poorly; incorrectly
maldito cursed; **¡maldita sea!** curses! darn it!
maleta bag, valise
malo (mal) bad; poor; **lo — es que** the worst (the joke) of it is that; **esa mala amiga** that disloyal friend
Mallorca or **Majorca** the largest island of the Balearic group off Spain's eastern coast. A Spanish possession
mamá mama, mother; **su señora** — your (dear) mother
Manacor a Spanish town and summer resort in Mallorca
mandar to order
manera manner, way; **de — que** so that; **¡de qué —!** and how!
mano *f.* hand
mantequilla butter
mañana tomorrow; **por la** — in the morning; **de** — early
maquillarse to put on makeup
maquinal mechanical
mar *m.* and *f.* sea; (*coll.*) a lot, lots
maravilloso marvellous
marcado marked; **— acento** strong accent
marchar to march; to proceed; **marcharse** to leave
marchito faded, withered
marido husband
Marsella or **Marseilles** a cosmopolitan city and France's greatest seaport
más more, most; rather; **— que** more than; **— de** (+ number) more than; **no — que** only, no more than; **sin — ni —** without much ado; at the slightest provocation
matar to kill
maternidad maternity
matrimonio marriage
mayor older; greater; larger; **— que** older than; **persona** — grown-up
mecanógrafa typist; secretary
medio half, a half; **a media voz** in a whisper; **a media luz** with dim lights; *n., m.* middle, means; **en — de** in the middle (midst) of
mejor better; best; **lo** — the best (thing); **a lo** — when least expected, quite possibly
memoria memory; **de** — by heart
menor least, smallest, slightest
menos less; least; except; **por lo** — at least
mentir (ie) to lie; to deceive
mentira lie, falsehood; **parece** — it seems incredible
menudo small, little; (*coll.*) terrific, awful
merecer* to deserve, merit; **— la pena** to be worth while
mermelada marmalade, jam
mes *m.* month
mesa table
mesilla or **mesita** small table; **— de noche** dresser, night table
meterse to get into; **— en algo** to meddle in something; **— con (alguno)** to pick a quarrel (with someone)
miedo fear; **tener** — to be afraid, fear
mientras (que) meanwhile; while, during the time
mil *m.* one thousand
millón *m.* million
mimar to spoil, indulge
mimo pampering; fondness; **con** — fondly
mirada glance
miramiento consideration; prudence; **miramientos** precautions
mirar to look (at); to see, examine; **— fijamente** to stare; **mírame bien** take a close look at me; **la mira a los ojos** (he) looks into her eyes; **mirarse** to look at oneself or each other

mismo same; self, very; **el** (or **eso**) — the (very) same; **ahora** — just now, right now; **lo** — the same thing; **de sí** — of himself
mocosa *f.* youngster, kid
moda fashion, style
modelo model, style, dress
modernismo modernism; modern ways; up-to-date ideas
modesto modest; proper
modo way, manner; **de ningún** — under no circumstances; **de otro** — otherwise; **de** — **que** so that; **este** — **de ser mío** this nature of mine
mohín *m.* grimace, face; gesture; **un** — **de desdén** a sneer
mohino sad; peevish; fretful
molestar to molest, annoy; to tease; **molestarse** (**en**) to bother
molesto annoyed, vexed; uncomfortable
molido fatigued, worn out
momento moment; **en este** — at this moment
"**monsieur**" (*French*) Sir, Mr.
monstruo monster
moral moral; *n.* morality, ethics
moreno dark, brunette; *n.* a brunette
morir(**se**) (**ue**) to die
mortificado mortified, embarrassed
mostrar (**ue**) to show; to point out
motivo motive, reason
mover(**se**) (**ue**) to move; to shake (the head)
movimiento movement; gesture
muchacha girl; young lady
muchacho boy; young man
mucho much, a lot; **muchos** many
mueble *m.* piece of furniture; **muebles** furniture
muerto dead; (*p.p.* of **morir**) died; *n., m.* a dead man
mujer woman, lady; wife; **¡** — **!** my dear!; **¡ pero** — **!** but look here!
mundano worldly
mundo world; **todo el** — everybody; **hombre de** — man of experience
museo museum
músico musician
muy very; **la** — ... the big ...

N

nacer* to be born; **he nacido** I was born
nada nothing; — **más** only; **no** ... — not ... anything
nadie nobody, no one, not ... anyone; — **más** no one else
Napoleón Napoleon Bonaparte (1769–1821), Emperor of France and the greatest military genius of his day
natural natural; **lo** — the obvious thing
necesitar to need; to have to
negar (**ie**) to deny; **negarse a** (+ *inf.*) to refuse to
negro black
nervio nerve; **con los nervios rotos** with (her) nerves shattered
nervioso nervous
nevera ice box, refrigerator
ni nor, neither; not even; — **siquiera** not even; — ... — neither ... nor; — **más** — **menos** nothing less
ninguno (**ningún**) none, no one, not ... any
niño boy, child
noche *f.* night; **esta** — tonight; **toda una** — a whole night; **de** — at night; **buenas noches** good night
nombre *m.* name
notar to notice; to guess
noventa ninety
novia bride; fiancée; sweetheart; girl friend
nuevo new; **de** — again
nunca never; **no** ... — never, not ... ever; **más que** — more than ever

O

o or, either
obligar* a to compel, oblige
observar to observe
obvio obvious
ocasión occasion, opportunity
ocultar to hide

ocupar to occupy; **ocuparse** (**de**) to busy oneself, attend to; **estar ocupado** to be busy
ocurrencia occurrence, event; idea; **una buena** — a good idea
ocurrido occurred, happened; **lo** — what happened, the event
ocurrir to occur, happen; **¿ qué le ocurre ?** what's the matter?; **se les ocurre la idea** they come up with the idea
odiar to hate
ofender to offend; to hurt (another's vanity); **ofenderse** to be (feel) offended
ofrecer* to offer; **ofrecerse a** to offer to
oir* to hear, listen; **¡ oiga !** look here!
ojo eye; **con los ojos bajos** with downcast eyes; **buscar con los ojos** to look around
olvidar(**se**) **de** to forget
opinar to judge; **¿ qué opinas ?** what is your opinion?
orden *f.* order, instructions
ordenanza *m.* orderly; bell boy
ordenar to arrange, order
ordinariez *f.* rough manner; insult; vulgarity
ordinario ordinary, common, vulgar; mean
orgullo pride
orgulloso proud
oscuro dark; **a oscuras** — in the dark
otro other, another; — **hombre** a different man

P

padecer* to suffer
padre father; **padres** parents; — **de familia** head of the family
país *m.* country, nation
palabra word; (*coll.*) **¡ — !** honest! my word of honor!
paliza beating, cudgelling
Palma the largest city in the island of Mallorca, and a popular tourist resort
palmotear to clap hands, applaud
Pamplona the capital of the Spanish province of Navarre, considered highly conservative in politics and religion
pan *m.* bread
pantalón *m.* trouser; (generally plural) **pantalones** trousers, slacks
Papa (**El**) the Pope
papá *m.* papa, father
papel *m.* paper; part, role (in a play); **papelito** scrap of paper; note
par *m.* pair; couple
para for; to, in order to; so that; — **no** so as not to; — **que** so that; **¿ — qué ?** for what purpose ? why? **como** — so as to
parar to stop
parecer* to appear, seem; **al** — apparently; — **mentira** to seem incredible; **me pareces otra** you seem like a different person (to me); **¿ qué te parece?** what do you think of him (it)?
París Paris, capital of France
parte *f.* part; **ninguna** — nowhere, not ... anywhere; **a** (**por**) **todas partes** everywhere; **por su** — on your (his) behalf
pasado past, last; **el verano** — last summer; — **de moda** out of style
pasar to happen; to pass; to spend (time); **lo que pasa es** the trouble is; **¿ qué pasa ?** what's wrong?
pasear(**se**) to take a walk, stroll; to pace
paseo walk; **dar un** — to take a walk; **paseíto** (*dim.*) a little walk
pasillo hallway
pasión passion; love
paso step; — **a** — step by step
patada kick
pavor *m.* fear, terror
paz *f.* peace; **y en** — and that's that; and that's all
pecado sin
pécora (*coll.*) designing woman
pedir (**i**) to ask, ask for, beg, request; — **relaciones** to propose

pegar* to hit, strike; to stick; **no — un ojo** not to sleep a wink; **— un respingo** to jump up suddenly; **— un puñetazo** to bring one's fist down; **— un grito** to scream
peinar(**se**) to comb (one's hair)
película film, movie
peligro danger; **poner en —** to endanger
peligroso dangerous
pelo hair
peluquería barber shop; beauty parlor
pena pain; sorrow, grief; **merecer la —** to be worth while
pendencia quarrel, fight
pensado: ser mal — to have a suspicious mind
pensamiento thought
pensar (**ie**) to think, think over, consider; **— en** to think about; **pensarlo bien** to think the matter over carefully
pensión boarding house
peor worse; worst
pequeño small, little; *n.*, *m.* little one
perder (**ie**) to lose; to waste (time); to miss
perdón *m.* pardon; **¡ — !** pardon me!
perdonar to pardon, forgive, excuse
perezoso lazy; **¡ valiente — !** you lazy bones!
peripuesto (*coll.*) spruced up
perla pearl
permiso permission; **con —** pardon me; with your permission
permitir to permit
pero but
persona person; **— mayor** adult, grown-up
personaje *m.* character (of a play); person
pertenencia ownership, possession; **un vestido de su —** a dress of hers
pesar *m.* grief, sorrow; **a — de** in spite of
pescar* to fish; (*coll.*) to catch (i.e., a cold)
peseta Spanish coin greatly reduced in value in the last fifty years and worth at present about two cents in American money
pésimo very bad
piadoso merciful; **piadosamente** pleadingly
picado hurt, piqued
picardía roguery; mean trick
pie *m.* foot; **ponerse en —** to stand up; **ir a —** to walk
pieza room; fragment
pijama *m.* pajamas
pillar to catch; **— el truco** to catch (someone) at a trick
pillería rascality
pintar to paint
pintura painting; **— de vanguardia** "ultra-modern" painting
piropear (*coll.*) to flatter, pay compliments
piropo compliment
piso floor
pizca (*coll.*) bit; **¡ ni — !** not a bit!
planta plant
plantarse to pose, stand squarely
pleito lawsuit
pleno full; **en plena crisis** at the height of a nervous crisis
plumero feather duster
pobre poor; miserable; **— de mí** poor me; **la pobrecilla** the poor thing
poco little; **al —** shortly after; **— a —** gradually; **pocos** few
poder* (**ue**) to be able, can; **no — con** to be unable to cope with; **no lo puedo remediar** I can't help it; **no puedo más** I can't stand it any longer; **¿ se puede?** may I come in?
Policía *f.* police
ponerse* to put on; to get, become; **— a** to begin to; **— de mal genio** to get angry; **— en medio** to get in the way; **— de pie** to stand up
Pontejos, calle de Pontejos Street
por by, for, through, because of; along; **— fortuna** fortunately; **— ciento** per cent; **— supuesto** of course; **— eso** for that reason; **— mí** as far as I'm concerned

porque because; **¿ por qué?** why?
¡ porras ! (*coll.*) darn it!; **¡ a la porra !** the devil with it!
portal *m.* entrance, porch
portarse to behave
porte *m.* appearance
posada inn, hotel
poseer to possess, own
posible possible; **¿ será posible ?** can it be possible?
postal *f.* postal card
práctica practice; habit
Prado, Museo del a magnificent art museum in Madrid
precioso beautiful; darling
preciso exact, precise; necessary; **es —** it is necessary
preferir (**ie**) to prefer
pregunta question; **hacer una —** to ask a question
preguntar to ask, inquire; **eso no se pregunta** there is no need to ask that
prenda pledge; forfeit (in games)
preocupado worried, concerned
preocuparse to worry
preparar to prepare
prestigio prestige
presumido boastful, proud
presumir to presume, boast
presuroso hasty
pretender to pretend, claim; to want
prima cousin; **primita** (*dim.*) (dear) little cousin
primavera spring (season)
primero (**primer**) first; at first; **de primer año** elementary
primitivo primitive
primo cousin; **primos hermanos** first cousins
principio principle
prisa hurry, haste; **tener —** to be in a hurry
probar (**ue**) to try; to taste
procedimiento procedure, method
procurar to endeavor, try
producir* to produce
profesor *m.* professor, teacher
profundo profound, deep; **un beso —** a long kiss
prometer to promise
pronto soon, quickly; **de —** suddenly; **¡ — !** quick!
propio own
proponer* to propose; to suggest; to intend
proporción opportunity, chance
prorrumpir to break forth, burst forth
protestar to protest
provincia province; **en** (**de**) **provincias** in (or from) the provinces (referring to any town or place outside the big cities like Madrid)
prueba proof; trial; **hacer la —** to try, test
psch (*interjection*) oh! well!
pueblo people, nation
puerta door; **Puerta de Toledo** a "square" or crossroads in Madrid
pues well, well then
puesta setting; **— de largo** coming out party; "début"
puesto (*p.p.* of *poner*) placed, put; *n.*, *m.* place; position
¡ pum ! (*coll.*) bang!
punta point; end; **de — en blanco** all dressed up
puntapié *m.* kick (with tip of the shoe)
puntillas: de — on tiptoe
punto point; dot; **estar a —** to be ready, all set; **poner los puntos** (*coll.*) to speak frankly
puñetazo fistcuff; **dar puñetazos a alguien** to sock someone
puño fist; cuff

Q

qué what; how; **¡ — buena eres !** you're so good!; **¿ — ?** what? I beg your pardon?
quedar to remain, be left; **— en** to agree; **— agradecido** to be grateful; **quedarse** to stay, remain; to be
quemar to burn; **quemarse** to be burned

querer* to wish, want; to consent; to like, love; to will; — **decir** to mean; **sin** — unintentionally; **sin — hacer daño** without meaning any harm; **¿ te quieres callar ?** will you be quiet?
querido dear, beloved; *n.* my dear (fellow)
¡ quia ! huh!
quieto quiet, peaceful; **estése usted** — behave yourself
quietud *f.* tranquility, repose
quinientas five hundred
quitar to take away, take out, remove; **quitarse** to take off
quizá perhaps

R

rabia fury, anger; **dar** — to make (one) angry
ramo bouquet; bunch
rápido swift, quick; quickly
rato while, short while
razón *f.* reason; right; mind; **tener** — to be right; **con** — rightly so; **con santa** — with conviction; **cargado de** — fully confident of being right
realmente really, actually
recado message
recatado modest
recién recently, just; — **llegado** newly arrived
reciente recent
recitar to recite
recoger* to gather; — **las lágrimas** to wipe (away) one's tears
reconcentrado intense; vehement
reconocer* to recognize, realize; to confess, admit (one's faults)
reconquistar to reconquer
reconvención accusation, reproach; **con bondadosa** — gently reproachful
recordar (ue) to recall, remember
recorrer to examine; to wander (through the streets)
recuerdo souvenir, remembrance; **recuerdos** memories
recurrir to resort to
recurso recourse; **recursos** means, devices; **tiene recursos para todo** she has a way out for everything
redondo round
referirse (ie) a to refer to
reflexionar to reflect, consider
refugiarse to take refuge
refunfuñar to grumble, mutter
regañar to scold
regocijado joyful
regocijo joy
regresar to return
reir* (**i**) to laugh; **reirse de** (**alguien**) to laugh at (someone)
relación relation; **pedir relaciones** to propose
reloj *m.* watch, clock
remediar to remedy; to help
remedio remedy; help; **¡ qué — !** what else can I do! there's no help for it!
rendido worn out
rendirse to yield, submit
renunciar to renounce, give up
reñir* (**i**) to scold
reojo: de — furtive; furtively
reparto distribution; cast of characters
repentino sudden
repetir (**i**) to repeat
repiquetear to ring; to click (heel of shoe)
reposo tranquility, rest
representante *m.* representative
representar to represent; (theatre) to perform, act
requeteplanches: requete (emphatic) + **planches** (iron) that you iron very carefully
resignado resigned
resignarse to resign oneself; accept
resistir to stand, endure
respingo jump, start
respirar to breathe
resplandeciente glowing
resplandor *m.* radiance; light rays
responder to answer
responsable *m.* responsible one; the one to blame

resultar to result; to turn out (to be)
resumen *m.* summary, synthesis
retirarse to withdraw, retire
Retiro (**El**) the largest park in Madrid
retonto very stupid
rico rich; delicious; **¿ me oyes, rica ?** do you hear me, darling?
riendo laughing
río river
risa laughter
risueño smiling; agreeable; **muy —** very pleased; **con risueña impaciencia** with amused impatience
rodear to surround
rodilla knee; **— en tierra** on one knee
rogar (**ue**) to beg, ask
Rollo, calle del a street in Madrid
romper to break; to begin; **— en sollozos** to burst into tears
rosa rose
Rosaleda the rose gardens in El Retiro park
rostro face
roto broken, shattered
rozar* to graze; to touch
rubor *m.* blush; shame
ruborizado blushing
ruido noise

S

saber* to know, know how to, be able to; **¡ si supieras ... !** if you (only) knew ... !; **¿ sabes ?** you do understand?
Sacramento, calle del a typical street in the old section of Madrid
sacrificar* to sacrifice; **sacrificarse** to sacrifice oneself
sagrado sacred
Salamanca, barrio de one of the fashionable districts in Madrid
salir* to go out, leave, exit; to come out; to appear; to grow (a beard); **— de noche** to step out at night
salón *m.* parlor
saltar to jump
saludar to greet
salvaje *m.* savage
salvar to save; **salvarse** to save oneself
santa saintly; **con — razón** with conviction
satisfecho satisfied
secar* (**se**) to dry (oneself)
seco dry; **en —** suddenly
seguida: en — at once, immediately
seguido followed; successive; **— de** followed by
seguir* (**i**) to follow; to continue; **— con la mirada** to keep watching
segundo second
seguro sure, certain; of course; **estar —** to be sure, certain
sencillo simple; plain, natural
sensato sensible
sentado seated, sitting
sentar* (**ie**) to become; to suit; **sentarse** to sit down
sentido sense; feeling; **doble —** double meaning
sentimiento sentiment, feeling; regret
sentir (**ie**) to feel; to regret, be sorry; **¡ cómo lo siento !** how sorry I am!; **sentirse** (**mal**) to feel (ill)
señalar to point out, indicate
señor man, gentleman; Mr.; Sir; master; **¡ el señor !** the master!
señora lady; woman; madam; Mrs.; lady of the house (or mistress)
señorita Miss; young lady; young girl
señorito young gentleman, Master
separar to separate
ser* to be; **¿ es que ... ?** is it possible (that) ... ?; **es que** the fact is, it's merely that ... ; *n.*, *m.* existence; a being
serenidad serenity, tranquility
serio serious; dignified; proper
Serrano, calle de Serrano Street
servicio service
servir (**i**) to serve
si if; whether; why; but
sí yes; of course; certainly; **— es** (it) certainly is; **eso —** to be sure; **creo que —** I think so; **— que** (+ clause) certainly, truly

siempre always; — **que** whenever; **como** — as usual
Siglo de Oro the Golden Age or Renaissance period (1450–1650) of Spanish art and thought
significar* to signify, mean
Sigüenza a Spanish town N. E. of Madrid, noted for its magnificent cathedral
siguiendo following; — **por ese camino** if they continue that way
siguiente next, following
silbar to whistle
silla chair
sillón *m.* easy chair; armchair
simpatía charm; congeniality; attraction; **sentir — por alguien** to find someone charming; to like or feel congenial toward someone
simpático pleasant, nice, likable, attractive
sin without; — **más ni más** without further ado
sinceridad sincerity; frankness
sino but; except; **no** ... — only
sinvergüenza *m.* scoundrel; a shameless one
siquiera even; scarcely; **ni** — not even
sitio place, spot
situación situation; circumstance; position
situar to place, locate; **situarse** to settle (station) oneself in a place
soberbia excessive pride; haughtiness
sobre on, upon; — **todo** especially, above all
sobresaltado startled
sobresalto sudden start; fear
sobrina niece
socialdemocracia Social Democracy (a political philosophy of the Socialist type)
sofocar* to smother, stifle
sol *m.* sun; (*coll.*) **¡ es un — !** he (she) is a doll!
solapa lapel
solemnidad solemnity; **con** — solemnly
solícito solicitous, concerned
solo alone; only; **a solas** all alone; **a mí solita** just to me
sólo only
soltar (**ue**) to let go; to set free; to drop; — **una bofetada** to punch
soltero bachelor
sollozo sob
sombra shadow
sombrero hat
sonreir (**i**) to smile
sonriedo smiling
sonrisa smile
soñador *m.* dreamer; (*coll.*) up in the clouds
soñar (**ue**) to dream; — **con** (**alguien**) to dream about (someone)
sopapo (*coll.*) blow, slap
¡ sopla ! (*coll.*) golly! (the context would indicate a stronger slang expression)
soportar to suffer, endure, bear
sorbo sip, swallow
sorprendido surprised; taken aback
sorpresa surprise
sosiego tranquility, calm; **respirar con** — to breathe easily
sospecha suspicion
sospechar to suspect
sostener* to maintain, uphold; keep up
suave soft; delicate, gentle
suavidad gentleness; forbearance
súbito sudden; suddenly
sublime sublime; superior
suceder to happen; **¿ qué sucede ?** what's wrong?
sudamericano South American
sudor *m.* sweat, perspiration
suelo floor
sueño dream; sleep
suerte *f.* luck, good luck; fate; **¡ qué suerte tienes !** how lucky you are!
suficiente sufficient, enough; capable, competent; **muy** — very self-assured
sufrir to suffer, endure; to undergo (a change)
sugerencia suggestion
sugestionado influenced; hypnotized

suplicar* to beg
suponer* to suppose
supuesto: por — of course
surgir* to appear, come out
suspenso in suspense; **se quedan suspensos** they stop astonished
suspirar to sigh
suspiro sigh
susto fright, scare, fear; **de —** from fright

T

¡ ta ! (*coll.*) tut, tut!
taberna tavern, cabaret
tal such, such a; **— como** exactly as, just as
también also, too
tampoco neither; not ... either; **no ... —** not that either; **yo —** neither do I
tan so, as; such, such a; **— ... como** as (so) ... as
tanto so much; **— como** as much as, as well as; **tantos** so many
tararear to hum (a tune)
tarde late; *n., f.* afternoon; **por la —** in the afternoon
tarea task
taza cup
té *m.* tea
técnico technical; professional
techo ceiling
telefonear to telephone
teléfono telephone; **llamar por —** to telephone
telón *m.* curtain
temblar (ie) to tremble
tender (ie) to stretch, stretch out; to extend (the hand)
tener* to have, possess; **— que** (+ *inf.*) to have to; **— prisa** to be in a hurry; **— lástima (de)** to be sorry for; **— celos** to be jealous; **tiene que haber otro** there must be another one
teniente *m.* first lieutenant
tercero (tercer) third
terminar to finish, end, complete; **— de** (+ *inf.*) to finish (+ -ing form)
término end, ending; **primer —** foreground
ternura tenderness; **con —** tenderly
tesoro treasure; darling (as a term of endearment)
tía aunt; **tiita** (*dim.*) auntie
tiempo time; **a —** on time; **a un —** at once; **al (mismo) —** at the same time
tierra earth, world; ground; earth
timidez *f.* timidity
tinta ink; **de buena —** on good authority
tío uncle
típico typical, characteristic
tipo type
tirar to throw; to attract; **— de** to pull, attract
titular(se) to call; to be called, be entitled
título title; heading; **a — de broma** under the pretext of a joke
toalla towel
tocar* to touch; to play (a musical instrument)
todavía still, yet; nevertheless; all the time; **— no** not yet
todo all, whole; every; everything; **sobre —** above all, especially; **a todas horas** all the time, constantly
toldo awning
Toledo historically, one of Spain's most important cities, since it was formerly the capital of the Spanish kingdom, and also one of Spain's most beautiful cities, artistically and architecturally
tomar to take; to have; to drink; **¿ por quién me tomas ?** what do you take me for? **¡ toma !** well! not really!
tontería foolishness, nonsense; **hacer una —** to commit a blunder; **no diga usted tonterías** don't be absurd
tonto stupid, foolish; **retonto** very stupid; *n.* fool
torno: en — around, round about

torpe dull, awkward
torpeza stupidity, mistake
total total; result; in short, to sum up
tozudo stubborn
traer* to bring; to carry; to have; to wear; **trae el sombrero puesto** he is wearing his hat
traje *m.* dress, gown; suit; outfit
trampa trap, snare; **hacer —** to cheat
tranquilizar(se)* to quiet down
tranquilo calm, quiet, easy; **estar —** to be reassured, to be satisfied; **tan —** as calm as you please; **dormir —** to sleep in peace
transcurso course (of time)
transfigurar(se) to transform; to be transformed
transformar to transform
transición transition; sudden change in tone or manner (of the actor)
transportado overcome
tras (de) after, behind
trasnochador *m.* night owl
tratar (de) to try; to handle; **tratarse de** to be concerned with
travieso mischievous; naughty
tren *m.* train
triste sad
triunfar to triumph; to conquer
tromba waterspout; **entra como una —** she comes in like a whirlwind
tropel *m.* crowd, confusion; **en —** tumultuously, all at once
tropezar* **(ie)** to stumble; to meet accidentally
truco (*coll.*) trick
tumbado (*coll.*) sprawled

U

ufano proud
último last, final
único only, sole, solitary; **lo —** the only thing
Universitaria: ciudad — the (Madrid) university campus

V

vagabundo vagabond, hobo
valer* to be worth; **no — nada** to be worthless; **eso no vale** that's not fair
valiente brave, courageous; **¡ — perezoso!** (*coll.*) lazy bones!
valor *m.* value, valor
vanguardia vanguard; "ultramodern" (referring to art and literature)
varios several; different
vaso glass
veinte twenty; **a los — años (de casados)** after twenty years of marriage
velada evening party or gathering
Velázquez, calle de Velazquez Street
veloz swift
venir* to come
ver* to see; **a —** let's see; **tú verás** that's right; **se ve** that's obvious; **ya verás** you will see; **bien lo veo** I'm well aware of it
verano summer
veras: de — truly, really; **¿ de — ?** really? honestly?
verdad truth; true; **de —** truly, really; **¿ (no) (es) verdad ?** is that so? isn't that so?
verdadero true; actual; genuine
verde green
vergüenza shame; disgrace; **¡ qué — (tengo) !** how ashamed I am!; **dar —** to be (feel) ashamed
Versailles city in northern France near Paris, famous for its magnificent palace built by Louis XIV
verso verse; **hacer versos** to write poetry
vestíbulo hall, lobby
vestido dressed; *n.* dress
vestir (i) to dress; to wear
vez *f.* time, occasion; **otra —** again; **en — de** instead of; **por primera —** for the first time; **alguna —** sometime(s); **cada —** each time
viaje *m.* trip; **de —** on a trip; **hacer un —** to take a trip

vida life
viejo old; ancient; **de la vieja escuela** of the old-fashioned school
vigilar to watch (over); to look out (for)
vilo: en — in the air, in suspense; **tener en — al marido** to keep the husband dangling
vino wine
visita guest; visit
visitar to visit
visto seen; **está —** it is obvious; **por lo —** apparently
vivienda dwelling
vivir to live; (*coll.*) **¡ vivo !** so there ! so help me!
volubilidad fickleness
voluntad will
volver (**ue**) to turn; to return, come back; **— a** (+ *inf.*) to ... again; **— la espalda** to turn one's back; **volverse** to turn around; **volverse loco** to go out of one's mind
voz *f.* voice; **a media —** in a whisper; **en — baja** in a low voice; **sin —** speechless; **a voces** shouting
vuelta turn; return; **a la —** on (one's) return; **a la — de algo** on the way back from something; **— de espaldas** (her) back turned
vuelto returned

Y

ya already; now; soon; finally; **¡ — !** of course! I see! indeed! all right!; **— no** no longer; **— sé** I well know; **— ves** you can see for yourself; **— está** it's finished now; **— que** as long as
yendo (*pres. part.* of *ir*) going
yergue from *erguir*

Z

zapatilla slipper
zapato shoe
Zarauz a fashionable summer resort near San Sebastián (northern coast of Spain)
¡ zas ! (*coll.*) bang!